OGC Portfolio Product

Service Offerings and Agreements
ITIL® V3 Intermediate Capability Handbook

*it*SMF International
The IT Service Management Forum

London: TSO

information & publishing solutions

Published by TSO (The Stationery Office)
and available from:

Online
www.tsoshop.co.uk

Mail, Telephone, Fax & E-mail
TSO
PO Box 29, Norwich, NR3 1GN
Telephone orders/General enquiries:
0870 600 5522
Fax orders: 0870 600 5533
E-mail: customer.services@tso.co.uk
Textphone 0870 240 3701

TSO@Blackwell and other Accredited Agents

Customers can also order publications from:
TSO Ireland
16 Arthur Street, Belfast BT1 4GD
Tel 028 9023 8451 Fax 028 9023 5401

The Swirl logo™ is a Trade Mark of the Office of
Government Commerce

ITIL® is a Registered Trade Mark of the Office of
Government Commerce in the United Kingdom and
other countries

PRINCE® is a Registered Trade Mark of the Office of
Government Commerce in the United Kingdom and
other countries

PRINCE2™ is a Trade Mark of the Office of Government
Commerce

M_o_R® is a Registered Trade Mark of the Office of
Government Commerce in the United Kingdom and
other countries

MSP® is a Registered Trade Mark of the Office of
Government Commerce in the United Kingdom and
other countries

The ITIL endorsement logo™ is a Trade Mark of the
Office of Government Commerce

A CIP catalogue record for this book is available from
the British Library

A Library of Congress CIP catalogue record has been
applied for

First published 2010

ISBN 9780113312702 Single copy ISBN
ISBN 9780113312719 (Sold in a pack of 10 copies)

Printed in the United Kingdom by The Stationery Office,
London
P002386043   c8   11/10

Contents

4 Contents

Acknowledgements

AUTHORS

Alison Cartlidge, Steria, UK

Janaki Chakravarthy, independent consultant, UK

ADDITIONAL CONTENT

Ashley Hanna, HP, UK

REVIEWERS

Luci Allen, Pink Elephant, UK

Aidan Lawes, service management evangelist, UK

Tricia Lewin, independent consultant, UK

Trevor Murray, The Grey Matters, UK

Michael Imhoff Nielsen, IBM, Denmark

Sue Shaw, Tricentrica, UK

HP Suen, The Hong Kong Jockey Club

EDITORS

Alison Cartlidge, Steria, UK

Mark Lillycrop, itSMF UK

About this guide

This guide provides a quick reference to the processes covered by the ITIL® service offerings and agreements (SOA) syllabus. It is designed to act as a study aid for students taking the ITIL Capability qualification for SOA, and as a handy portable reference source for practitioners who work with these processes.

This guide is not intended to replace the more detailed ITIL publications, nor to be a substitute for a course provider's training materials. Many parts of the syllabus require candidates to achieve competence at Bloom levels 3 and 4, showing the ability to apply their learning and analyse a situation. This study aid focuses on the core knowledge that candidates need to acquire at Bloom levels 1 and 2, including knowledge and comprehension of the material that supports the syllabus.

For further syllabus details, see the current syllabus published by the APM Group at www.itil-officialsite.com.

Listed below in alphabetical order are the ITIL service management processes with cross-references to the publication in which they are primarily defined, and where significant further expansion is provided. Most processes play a role during each lifecycle stage, but only significant references are included. Those processes and functions specifically relevant to the SOA syllabus and covered in this guide are also listed. Abbreviations are given in full in section 1.2.

ITIL service management processes

Service management process	SOA syllabus	Primary source	Further expansion
Seven-step improvement process		CSI	
Access management		SO	
Availability management		SD	CSI
Capacity management		SD	SO, CSI
Change management		ST	
Demand management	✔	SS	SD
Evaluation		ST	
Event management		SO	
Financial management	✔	SS	
Incident management		SO	CSI
Information security management		SD	SO
IT service continuity management		SD	CSI
Knowledge management		ST	CSI
Problem management		SO	CSI
Release and deployment management		ST	SO
Request fulfilment		SO	

Service management process	SOA syllabus	Primary source	Further expansion
Service asset and configuration management		ST	SO
Service catalogue management	✔	SD	SS
Service level management	✔	SD	CSI
Service measurement		CSI	
Service portfolio management	✔	SS	SD
Service reporting		CSI	
Service validation and testing		ST	
Service strategy (strategy generation)		SS	
Supplier management	✔	SD	
Transition planning and support		ST	
Function			
Application management		SO	
IT operations management		SO	
Service desk		SO	
Technical management		SO	

1 Introduction to service management

Note that references in the headings are to section numbers in the ITIL core publications, where more detail can be found.

1.1 GOOD PRACTICE

Organizations operating in dynamic environments need to improve their performance and maintain competitive advantage. Adopting good practices in industry-wide use can help to improve capability.

There are several sources for good practice:

- **Public frameworks and standards** These have been validated across diverse environments; knowledge is widely distributed among professionals; there is publicly available training and certification; acquisition of knowledge through the labour market is easier
- **Proprietary knowledge of organizations and individuals** This is customized for the local context and specific business needs; may only be available under commercial terms; may be tacit knowledge (inextricable and poorly documented).

1.2 THE ITIL FRAMEWORK

The ITIL framework is a source of good practice in service management. The ITIL library has the following components:

- **ITIL core** Best-practice publications applicable to all types of organizations that provide services to a business
- **ITIL complementary guidance** A complementary set of publications with guidance specific to industry sectors, organization types, operating models and technology architectures.

The objective of the ITIL service management framework is to provide services for customers that are fit for purpose, stable and so reliable that the business views the IT service provider as a trusted partner. ITIL offers good-practice guidance applicable to all types of organization that provide IT services to businesses. The framework is neither bureaucratic nor unwieldy if utilized sensibly and in full recognition of the business needs of the organization.

ITIL has been deployed successfully around the world for more than 20 years. Over this time, the framework has evolved from a specialized set of service management topics with a focus on function, to a process-based framework, which now provides a broader holistic service lifecycle.

> **Definition: service lifecycle**
>
> The service lifecycle is an approach to IT service management that emphasizes the importance of coordination and control across the various functions, processes and systems necessary to manage the full lifecycle of IT services. The service management lifecycle approach considers the strategy, design, transition, operation and continual improvement of IT services.

The service lifecycle is described in a set of five publications within the ITIL core set. Each of these publications covers a stage of the service lifecycle (see Figure 1.1), from the initial definition and analysis of business requirements in *Service Strategy* (SS) and *Service Design* (SD), through migration into the live environment within *Service Transition* (ST), to live operation and improvement in *Service Operation* (SO) and *Continual Service Improvement* (CSI).

Figure 1.1 The service lifecycle

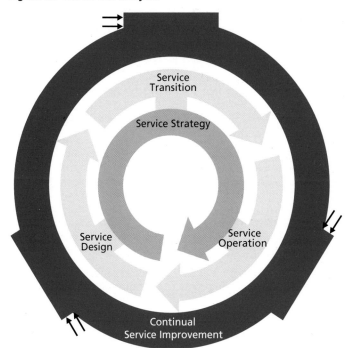

1.3 WHAT IS SERVICE MANAGEMENT? (SS 2.1–2.2, ST 2.1–2.2)

To understand what service management is, we need to understand what services are, and how service management can help service providers to deliver and manage these services.

Definition: service

A service is a means of delivering value to customers by facilitating outcomes that customers want to achieve without the ownership of specific costs and risks.

The outcomes that customers want to achieve are the reason why they purchase or use a service. The value of the service to the customer is directly dependent on how well a service facilitates these outcomes.

Service management is what enables a service provider to understand the services they are providing; to ensure that the services really do facilitate the outcomes their customers want to achieve; to understand the value of the services to their customers; and to understand and manage all of the costs and risks associated with those services.

Definition: service management

Service management is a set of specialized organizational capabilities for providing value to customers in the form of services.

These 'specialized organizational capabilities' are described in this guide, as they relate to SOA. They include the processes, activities, functions and roles that a service provider uses to enable it to deliver services to its customers, as well as the ability to organize, manage knowledge and understand how to facilitate outcomes that create value.

Service management is concerned with more than just delivering services. Each service, process or infrastructure component has a lifecycle, and service management considers the entire lifecycle from strategy through design and transition to operation and continual improvement.

1.4 SERVICE MANAGEMENT VALUE CREATION

1.4.1 Service value creation (SS 3.1)

An IT service provider has a set of assets in the form of capabilities and resources that it uses to create IT services for its customers. Each of its customers also has its own assets (resources and capabilities) and uses IT services to enable those customer assets to generate business value.

A customer of the IT service provider only perceives value from the IT services it receives if a direct connection can be made between the IT service and the business value it needs to generate. Therefore, it is essential that IT service providers focus on understanding, articulating and measuring how effective their services are in enabling their customers to achieve their desired outcomes. It is also important that the IT service provider acknowledges that there is frequently a difference between what the customer perceives as valuable and what the IT organization believes it provides.

Understanding the business outcomes and associated business values that are important to the customer is critical to the success of the IT service provider and can enable the service provider to differentiate itself from other providers.

To ensure a common understanding of these values, it is important that the value of a service is fully described in terms of utility (increase in performance of customer assets leading to increased outcomes) and warranty (decrease in potential performance variation). This can change customer perceptions of uncertainty in the promised benefits of a service.

Customers value an IT service when they see a clear relationship between that IT service and the business value they need to generate. The degree of value each customer perceives from an IT service is made up of two components: service utility and service warranty.

> **Definition: service utility**
>
> Service utility is the functionality of an IT service from the customer's perspective. The business value of an IT service is created by the combination of the service utility (what the service does) and service warranty (how well it does it).

Utility can be framed to support the business strategies of customers, in terms of business outcomes supported and associated business constraints removed – e.g. secure operational business processes supported without any constraints relating to business user location.

> **Definition: service warranty**
>
> Service warranty is the assurance that an IT service will meet agreed requirements. This may be a formal agreement such as a service level agreement (SLA) or contract, or a marketing message or brand image. The business value of an IT service is created by the combination of the service utility (what the service does) and service warranty (how well it does it).

Warranty can be communicated in terms of levels of certainty, i.e. the availability, capacity, continuity and security of the utilization of services.

Utility and warranty are not optional components. Both must exist for an IT service to provide value to the customer. Value creation is the combined effect of utility and warranty, where variations in either can be used to differentiate service providers, improving their value propositions and creating competitive advantage.

1.4.2 Service strategy value to the business

Any investment in service strategy must deliver business value in return. These benefits typically encompass:

- Improved use of IT investments
- Tight coupling between the perception of business and IT value
- Performance and measures that are business-value-based
- Service development investment decisions driven by business priorities and clear return on investment (ROI) plans
- Agile adaptation of IT services to pre-empt and meet changing business needs
- Clear visibility of linkages between business services and IT service assets.

1.4.3 Service design value to the business (SD 2.4.3)

The following benefits result from good service design:

- Improved consistency across all services and better integration with infrastructure components, leading to faster and simpler implementation, and improved quality of service
- Clear alignment with business needs, demonstrated through a focus on IT measurements directly related to key aspects of business performance
- More effective and relevant processes, with improved measurement methods and metrics, enabling informed decision making.

1.4.4 Service transition value to the business (ST 2.4.3)

Effective service transition provides the following benefits:

- Enables high volumes of change and release for the business
- Provides an understanding of the level of risk during and after change, e.g. service outage, disruption
- Aligns new or changed services with the customer's business requirements
- Ensures that customers and users can use the new or changed service effectively.

1.4.5 Service operation value to the business (SO 2.4.3)

Service operation is the stage in the lifecycle where the plans, designs and optimizations are executed and measured. Service operation is where actual value is seen by the business. The value provided to the business by service operation includes:

- Agreed levels of service delivered to the business and customers
- Optimization of the cost and quality of services.

1.4.6 Continual service improvement value to the business (CSI 3.7.2)

CSI recognizes that the value it provides to the business can be realized and measured in different ways:

- **Improvements** Outcomes that are favourably improved when compared to a 'before' state
- **Benefits** The gains achieved through realization of improvements
- **ROI** The difference between the benefit and the cost to achieve it

■ **Value on investment (VOI)** The extra value created by the establishment of benefits that include non-monetary outcomes.

Service measurement provides value to the business by enabling it to:

■ Validate previous decisions
■ Set direction in order to hit targets
■ Justify that a course of action is required
■ Intervene and take corrective action.

1.5 THE ITIL SERVICE MANAGEMENT MODEL

All services should be driven by business needs and requirements. Within this context they must also reflect the strategies and policies of the service provider organization, as indicated in Figure 1.2.

Figure 1.2 illustrates how the service lifecycle is initiated from a change in requirements in the business. These requirements are identified and agreed at the service strategy stage within a service level package (SLP) and a defined set of business outcomes.

This passes to the service design stage where a service solution is produced together with a service design package (SDP) containing everything necessary to take this service through the remaining stages of the lifecycle.

Figure 1.2 Key links, inputs and outputs of the service lifecycle stages

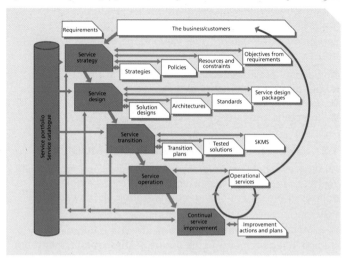

The SDP passes to the service transition stage, where the service is evaluated, tested and validated, and the service is transitioned into the live environment, where it enters the service operation stage.

Service operation focuses on providing effective and efficient operational services to deliver the required business outcomes and value to the customer.

Continual service improvement identifies opportunities for improvement anywhere within any of the lifecycle stages, based on measurement and reporting of the efficiency, effectiveness, cost-effectiveness and compliance of services, service management processes and technology.

The ITIL lifecycle uses models to refine and customize an organization's use of the ITIL practices. These models are intended to be re-usable in a variety of organizational contexts and to help take advantage of economies of scale and efficiencies.

Central to these models are the overarching process elements that interact throughout the lifecycle.

1.6 FUNCTIONS AND PROCESSES ACROSS THE SERVICE LIFECYCLE (SS 2.6, ST 2.3)

Definition: function

A team or group of people and the tools they use to carry out one or more processes or activities – for example, the service desk.

Functions are self-contained with capabilities and resources necessary for their performance and outcomes. They provide structure and stability to organizations. Coordination between functions through shared processes is a common organizational design.

Definition: process

A process is a structured set of activities designed to accomplish a specific objective. It takes one or more defined inputs and turns them into defined outputs. A process may include any of the roles, responsibilities, tools and management controls required to reliably deliver the outputs. A process may define policies, standards, guidelines, activities and work instructions if they are needed.

Process definitions describe actions, dependencies and sequence. Processes have the following characteristics. They:

- Are **measurable**, in management terms such as cost and quality, and in practitioner terms such as duration and productivity
- Exist to deliver **specific results** that are identifiable and countable
- Have **customers** or **stakeholders** with expectations that must be met by the results that the process delivers
- Respond to **specific events** that act as triggers for the process.

Figure 1.3 shows the high-level basic flow of lifecycle process elements in the service management model.

Feedback and control between the functions and processes within and across the lifecycle elements enable the specialization and coordination necessary in the lifecycle approach. Whilst the dominant pattern is the sequential lifecycle, every element provides points for feedback and control.

Figure 1.4 shows the key processes defined by each publication and lifecycle stage.

1.7 SERVICE OFFERINGS AND AGREEMENTS SUPPORTING THE SERVICE LIFECYCLE (SS 5.1, 5.3, 5.5.1, SD 2.4.5)

The processes within service offerings and agreements (SOA) cannot be considered in isolation. These processes must be linked together, with clearly defined interfaces, to manage, design, support and maintain services, IT infrastructures, environments,

Figure 1.3 A high-level view of the ITIL service management process model

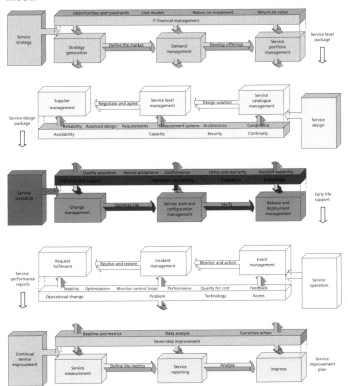

Figure 1.4 Service management processes across the service lifecycle

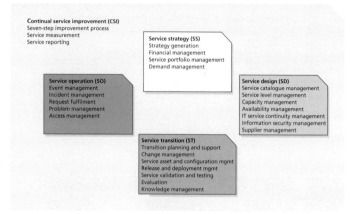

applications and data. It is imperative that roles and responsibilities are clearly defined when designing a service or process.

The processes detailed in this publication in support of SOA are as follows:

- **Service portfolio management** Manages the service portfolio in terms of the business value each service provides, governing service management investments across the enterprise
- **Service catalogue management** Ensures a service catalogue is produced and maintained for all services either being prepared or running operationally

- **Service level management** Negotiates, agrees and documents IT service targets, then monitors and produces reports on actual service performance during service operation
- **Demand management** Identifies business activity levels to support capacity planning and to enable actual demand to be influenced so that utilization is optimized
- **Supplier management** Manages suppliers and their services, ensuring seamless IT service quality and value for money
- **Financial management** Financially quantifies services, enabling budgeting, accounting, charging and decision making, strategically and operationally.

2   Service portfolio management

2.1   CONCEPTS (SS 5.3)

Service portfolio management (SPM) is a dynamic method of governing service management investments across the enterprise and managing them for value.

A service portfolio describes a provider's services in terms of business value, articulating business needs and the provider's response to those needs. As the basis for a decision framework, a service portfolio clarifies or helps to clarify the following strategic questions:

- Why should a customer buy these services?
- Why should they buy these services from us?
- What are the pricing or chargeback models?
- What are our strengths and weaknesses, priorities and risks?
- How should our resources and capabilities be allocated?

The term 'portfolio' may be marginalized to a list of services, applications, assets or projects. It is a set of investments that share similar characteristics, grouped by size, discipline or strategic value. There are a few fundamental differences between IT portfolio management, project portfolio management and SPM. All are enabling techniques for governance; the difference is in the implementation details.

Business services represent business activities with varying degrees of granularity and functionality, from an individual business process to a composite application, as defined by the business.

Business and IT services may differ by granularity or by context (technology versus business), but both provide a basis for value and require governance, delivery and support. IT service management (ITSM) and business service management (BSM) are two different perspectives on the same concept: service management.

IT priorities must be aligned with other drivers of business value. For IT to organize its activities around business objectives, the organization must link to business processes and services.

Organizations are moving from managing infrastructure, with a focus on component operational availability, to managing services centred on customer and business needs. The challenge is to derive operational objectives from business services and to manage accordingly. As business perspectives do not easily relate to IT infrastructure, BSM can be used to address this.

BSM is the ongoing practice of governing, monitoring and reporting on IT and the business service it impacts. It enables the service provider to manage business services by focusing its operations on business services to better align investments with business objectives. Key to BSM's effectiveness is the organization's ability to link service assets to its higher-level business services, based on causality instead of correlation, allowing infrastructure events to be tied to corresponding business outcomes.

The service portfolio is divided into three phases: service pipeline, service catalogue and retired services (see Figure 2.1).

Figure 2.1 Service pipeline and service catalogue

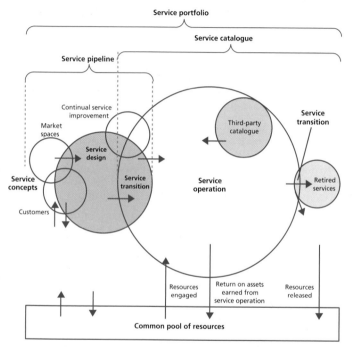

Area of circle is proportional to resources currently engaged in the lifecycle phase (service portfolio and financial management)

The service portfolio represents all the resources presently engaged or being released in various phases of the service lifecycle. This is a very important governance aspect of service portfolio management. Entry, progress and exit are approved only with agreed funding and a financial plan for recovering costs or showing profit as necessary. The portfolio needs to have the right mix of services in the pipeline and catalogue to secure the financial viability of the service provider. The service catalogue is the only part of the portfolio that recovers costs or earns profits.

The service catalogue is the subset of the service portfolio that is visible to customers. It consists of services active in the service operation phase and those approved to be offered to current or prospective customers. Items can enter the service catalogue only after due diligence has been performed on related costs and risks. Resources are engaged to fully support active services.

The service catalogue provides a service order and demand channelling mechanism. It acts as an acquisition portal for customers, with pricing and service-level commitments, plus terms and conditions, for service provisioning.

A subset of the service catalogue may be third-party or outsourced services that are offered to customers with varying levels of value addition or combination with other catalogue items. The third-party catalogue may consist of core service packages (CSP) and service level packages (SLP).

The service pipeline consists of services under development for a given market space or customer, representing the service provider's future growth and strategic outlook.

When services in the catalogue are phased out or retired, the related knowledge and information are stored in a knowledge base for future use.

2.2 PROCESS ACTIVITIES, METHODS AND TECHNIQUES (SS 5.4)

SPM, as a dynamic and ongoing process set, includes the following work methods:

- **Define** Inventory services, ensure business cases and validate portfolio data
- **Analyse** Maximize portfolio value, align and prioritize, and balance supply and demand
- **Approve** Finalize proposed portfolio, authorize services and resources
- **Charter** Communicate decisions, allocate resources and charter services.

2.2.1 Define

The 'define' phase collects information from all existing and all proposed services. Proposed services include those in a conceptual phase; i.e. all services an organization would do if it had unlimited resources, capabilities and time. This provides an understanding of the opportunity costs of the existing portfolio which helps to support subsequent analysis.

The cyclical nature of the SPM process means that this phase not only creates an initial inventory of services, but also validates the data on a recurring basis. Different portfolios will have different refresh cycles and validation needs to consider any changed circumstances; for example:

- Conditions and markets change, invalidating earlier ROI calculations
- Some services may no longer be optimal due to compliance or regulatory concerns
- Events such as mergers and acquisitions occur.

An efficient portfolio, with optimal levels of ROI and risk, maximizes the value realization for constrained and limited resources and capabilities.

Every service in the portfolio should include a business case. A business case is a model of what a service is expected to achieve. It is the justification for pursuing a course of action to meet stated organizational goals, acting as the link back to service strategy and funding. It is the assessment of a service investment in terms of potential benefits and the resources and capabilities required to provision and maintain it.

2.2.2 Analyse

The 'analyse' phase needs to be well defined prior to the 'define' phase to ensure the right data is collected to support the analysis.

Strategic intent is developed in this phase, by starting with a set of top-down questions which identify the perspective, position, plan and patterns:

- What are the long-term goals of the service organization?
- What services are required to meet those goals?
- What capabilities and resources are required for the organization to achieve those services?
- How will we get there?

The answers guide the analysis and the desired outcomes of SPM. Answering these questions requires the involvement of senior leaders and subject matter experts.

When considering the options, understanding the relationship between risks, impact and dependencies enables informed investment decisions in service initiatives to be made with appropriate levels of risk and reward. These initiatives may cross business functions and may span short, medium and longer timeframes. Moreover, the calculated value realization for each service investment should be commensurate with its level of risk.

Service investments are normally split between three strategic categories:

- **Run the business (RTB)** Investments centred on maintaining service operations
- **Grow the business (GTB)** Investments intended to grow the organization's scope of services
- **Transform the business (TTB)** Investments to move into new market spaces.

Investment categories are further divided into budget allocations:

- **Venture** Create services in a new market space
- **Growth** Create new services in existing market space
- **Discretionary** Provide enhancements to existing services
- **Non-discretionary** Maintain existing services
- **Core** Maintain business critical services.

A potentially large hidden cost for a service provider can be termination of services. A clear path is required for retiring redundant services. Since the cost of retiring a service may temporarily exceed that of maintaining it, its budget allocation can shift from non-discretionary to discretionary.

A useful tool for making decisions on the timing and sequencing of investments in a service portfolio is an option space; see Figure 2.2. An option space can guide decisions to invest and, if so, when. In addition to financial measures, other factors may also influence investment decisions; these include mission imperatives, compliance, trends, intangible benefits, strategic or business fit, social responsibilities and innovation.

Figure 2.2 Option space

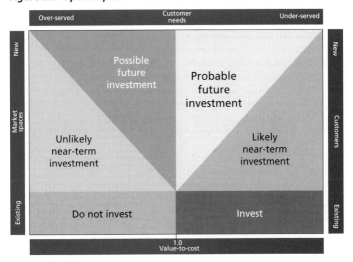

2.2.3   Approve

The previous phases have led to a well-understood future 'to be' state. In this phase approvals (with the corresponding authorization for new services and resources) or disapprovals of that future state take place. The outcomes for existing services fall into six categories:

■ **Retain** Services that are aligned with and relevant to the organization's strategy

■ **Replace** Services that have unclear and overlapping business functionality

- **Rationalize** Services that are composed of multiple releases of the same operating system, multiple versions of the same software and/or multiple versions of system platforms providing similar functions
- **Refactor** Services that meet the technical and functional criteria of the organization but display unclear process or system boundaries. Services can be refactored to include only the core functionality, with common services providing the remainder or where they have embedded re-usable business services
- **Renew** Services that meet functional fitness criteria, but fail on technical fitness
- **Retire** Services that do not meet minimum levels of technical and functional fitness.

2.2.4 Charter

The list of decisions and action items needs to be communicated clearly and unambiguously to the organization. These decisions should correlate to budgetary decisions and financial plans. Budget allocations enforce the allocation of resources.

The expected value of each service should be built into financial forecasts and resource plans, and tracked. Newly chartered services are promoted to service design. Existing services are refreshed in the service catalogue. Retired services begin their withdrawal through service transition.

2.3   INTERFACES (SS 4.2.3, 5.1.2.3)

The service portfolio interfaces with other phases and processes as follows:

- The service pipeline reflects the extent to which new service concepts and ideas for improvement are being fed by service strategy, service design and continual service improvement

- Service transition phases service pipeline services into operation following completion of design, development and testing, and retires other services, ensuring that all customer commitments are fulfilled and service assets are released from contracts
- The service catalogue is a subset of the service portfolio
- Service level management uses SPM's documentation of the organization's standardized services
- Financial management ensures adequate funding for the pipeline
- Financial management is a key input to SPM. It enables an organization to benchmark its service costs against other providers, and use IT financial information, combined with service demand and internal capability information, to make decisions on whether to provision services internally or externally
- The service portfolio includes ongoing service improvement plans initiated by continual service improvement.

3   Service catalogue management

3.1   PURPOSE/GOAL/OBJECTIVES (SD 4.1.1)

The purpose of service catalogue management is to provide a single source of consistent information on all agreed services and ensure that it is widely available to those who are approved to access it.

The goal of service catalogue management is to ensure a service catalogue is produced and maintained, containing accurate information on all operational services and those being prepared to be run operationally.

The objective of service catalogue management is to manage the information contained within the service catalogue, ensuring it is accurate and reflects the current details, status, interfaces and dependencies of all services that are being run, or being prepared to run, in the live environment.

3.2   SCOPE (SD 4.1.2)

The scope of service catalogue management is to provide and maintain accurate information on all services that are being transitioned or have been transitioned to the live environment.

Activities in scope include:

- Definition of the service
- Production and maintenance of an accurate service catalogue
- Management of interfaces, dependencies and consistency between the service catalogue and service portfolio
- Management of interfaces and dependencies between all services and supporting services within the service catalogue and the configuration management system (CMS)

■ Management of interfaces and dependencies between all services, and supporting components and configuration items (CIs) within the service catalogue and the CMS.

3.3 VALUE TO THE BUSINESS (SS 4.2.3, SD 3.10, 4.1.3)

The service catalogue provides a central source of information on the IT services delivered by the service provider organization, providing all areas of the business with an accurate, consistent view of the IT services, their details and status. It contains a customer-facing view of the IT services in use, how they are intended to be used, the business processes they enable, and the levels and quality of service the customer can expect for each service.

It acts as an acquisition portal for customers, including pricing, service level commitments, and terms and conditions for service provisioning.

Business service management (BSM) is a strategy and approach to enable IT components to be linked to the goals of the business. The service catalogue (including business units, processes and services, and their relationships with and dependencies on IT services, technology and components) is crucial to increasing the IT service provider's capability to deliver BSM, enabling it to predict the impact of technology on the business and how business change may impact technology.

3.4 POLICIES, PRINCIPLES AND BASIC CONCEPTS (SD 4.1.4, SD APPENDIX G)

Once a service is 'chartered' (i.e. being developed for use by customers), service design produces the specifications for the service, at which point the service is added to the service catalogue. The service catalogue contains a summary of each service, its characteristics and details of its customers and maintainers.

A CMS or any sort of asset database can provide valuable sources of information. These sources need to be verified before inclusion within either the service portfolio or service catalogue.

Figure 3.1 illustrates example contents for a service portfolio and service catalogue.

A policy is required for both the portfolio and catalogue, stating the services to be recorded within them, service details to be recorded and what statuses are recorded for each service. The policy also details responsibilities for each section of the portfolio and the scope of each of the constituent sections.

An organization needs to develop a policy defining what a service is and how it is defined and agreed within the organization.

There are two aspects to the service catalogue:

■ **Business service catalogue** The customer view of the service catalogue; contains details of the IT services delivered to the customer, with relationships with the business units and business processes that rely on the IT services
■ **Technical service catalogue** Underpins the business service catalogue and is not part of the customer view; contains details of all IT services delivered to the customer, including relationships with any supporting services, shared services, components and CIs necessary to support service provision to the business.

The business service catalogue facilitates the development of a proactive and pre-emptive SLM process, allowing it to develop BSM.

Figure 3.1 Example elements of a service portfolio and service catalogue

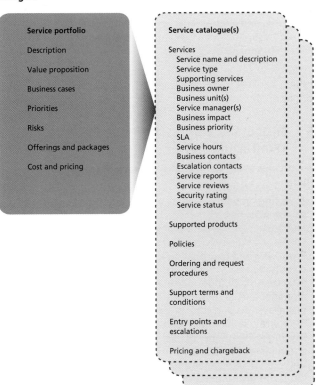

Service portfolio

Description

Value proposition

Business cases

Priorities

Risks

Offerings and packages

Cost and pricing

Service catalogue(s)

Services
    Service name and description
    Service type
    Supporting services
    Business owner
    Business unit(s)
    Service manager(s)
    Business impact
    Business priority
    SLA
    Service hours
    Business contacts
    Escalation contacts
    Service reports
    Service reviews
    Security rating
    Service status

Supported products

Policies

Ordering and request
procedures

Support terms and
conditions

Entry points and
escalations

Pricing and chargeback

The technical service catalogue helps when constructing the relationship between services, service level agreements (SLAs), operational level agreements (OLAs) and other underpinning agreements and components, as it identifies the technology required to support a service and the support group or groups for the components.

The business service catalogue and technical service catalogue combined are useful for assessing the impact of incidents and changes on the business.

3.5   PROCESS ACTIVITIES, METHODS AND TECHNIQUES (SD 4.1.5)

Key activities in the service catalogue management process include:

- Agreeing and documenting a service definition with all relevant parties
- Interfacing with service portfolio management to agree the contents of the service portfolio and service catalogue
- Producing and maintaining a service catalogue, in conjunction with the service portfolio
- Interfacing with business and IT service continuity management to identify and manage the dependencies of business units and their business processes on the supporting IT services contained in the business service catalogue
- Liaising with support teams, suppliers and configuration management to identify the interfaces and dependencies between IT services and supporting services, components and CIs in the technical service catalogue
- Interfacing with business relationship management and service level management to ensure that information is aligned to the business and business process.

3.6 TRIGGERS, INPUTS, OUTPUTS AND INTERFACES (SS 4.2.3, SD 3.6.2, 3.9, 3.10, SD 4.1.6)

Triggers for service catalogue management are changes in business requirements and services. Therefore key triggers are requests for change and the change management process, including new services, changes to existing services or services being retired.

Inputs include:

- Business information from an organization's business and IT strategy, plans and financial plans, and information on its current and future requirements from the service portfolio
- Business impact analysis, providing information on the impact, priority and risk associated with each service or changes to service requirements
- Details of any agreed, new or changed business requirements from the service portfolio; i.e. service pipeline items to be added to the service catalogue once chartered
- Service portfolio design requirements for the service catalogue
- The CMS
- Feedback from all other processes
- BSM to ensure the design of the catalogue supports BSM activities.

Outputs include:

- The documentation and agreement of a 'definition of the service'
- Updates to the service portfolio, including current status of all services and requirements for services
- The service catalogue, with details and current status for all live services provided or being transitioned into the live environment, plus interfaces and dependencies.

Interfaces include:

- Service strategy, as the service catalogue is the virtual projection of the service providers' actual and present capabilities
- Service portfolio management, as the service catalogue is an integral part of the service portfolio, communicating and defining the policies, guidelines and accountability required for SPM
- Service-oriented architecture, as the service catalogue shows the relationship between services and applications
- Demand management provides common patterns of business activity (PBA) to support clustering of catalogue items into lines of service
- Configuration management, as each service is defined as a CI, forming a service hierarchy in the CMS to support other SM processes
- All changes within the service portfolio and service catalogue are subject to change management
- The service catalogue can support other service management processes; for example, performing business impact analysis (BIA) within IT service continuity planning, or redistributing workloads, within capacity management
- Business relationship management and service level management to ensure that the information is aligned to the business and business process
- BSM, enabling impact assessments to take place between business and IT.

3.7 METRICS AND MEASUREMENT (SD 4.1.8)

The two main key performance indicators for service catalogue management are:

- The number of services recorded and managed within the service catalogue as a percentage of those being delivered and transitioned in the live environment
- The number of variances detected between the information contained within the service catalogue and the 'real world' situation.

3.8   ROLES AND RESPONSIBILITIES (SD 6.4.5)

The service catalogue manager has responsibility for producing and maintaining the service catalogue, including:

- Ensuring all operational services and all services being prepared for operational running are recorded within the service catalogue
- Ensuring all information in the service catalogue is accurate and up-to-date
- Ensuring all information in the service catalogue is consistent with the information within the service portfolio
- Ensuring the information in the service catalogue is adequately protected and backed up.

3.9   CHALLENGES, CRITICAL SUCCESS FACTORS AND RISKS (SD 4.1.9)

The major challenge facing service catalogue management is maintaining an accurate service catalogue as part of a service portfolio, incorporating both the business service catalogue and the technical service catalogue as part of an overall CMS and service knowledge management system.

Key critical success factors include:

- An accurate service catalogue
- Business users' awareness of the services being provided
- IT staff awareness of the technology supporting the services.

Risks associated with providing an accurate service catalogue include:

- Inaccuracy of the data in the catalogue and its not being under rigorous change control
- Poor acceptance of the service catalogue and its usage in all operational processes – the more active the catalogue is, the more likely it is to be accurate
- Inaccuracy of service information from the business, IT and service portfolio
- Lack of tools and resources required to maintain the information
- Poor access to accurate change management information and processes
- Poor access to, and support of, appropriate and up-to-date CMS and service knowledge management system
- Circumvention of use of the service portfolio and service catalogue
- Information is either too detailed to maintain accurately or too high-level to be of value.

4 Service level management

4.1 PURPOSE/GOAL/OBJECTIVES (SD 4.2.1)

The purpose of service level management (SLM) is to ensure that all operational services and their performance are measured in a consistent, professional manner throughout the IT organization, and that the services and reports produced meet the needs of the business and customers.

The goal of SLM is to ensure that an agreed level of IT service is provided for all current IT services, and that future services are delivered to agreed achievable targets.

The objectives of SLM are to:

- Define, document, agree, monitor, measure, report and review the level of IT services provided
- Provide and improve relationships and communication with the business and customers
- Ensure specific and measurable targets are developed for all IT services
- Monitor and improve customer satisfaction with the quality of services delivered
- Ensure IT and customers have a clear and unambiguous expectation of the level of service to be delivered
- Ensure proactive measures to improve levels of service delivered are implemented, wherever cost-justifiable.

4.2   SCOPE (SD 4.2.2)

SLM includes:

- Development of relationships with the business, providing a point of regular contact and communication, representing the IT service provider to the business and the business to the IT service provider
- Negotiation and agreement of current requirements and targets, and the documentation and management of service level agreements (SLAs) for all operational services
- Negotiation and agreement of future requirements and targets, and the documentation and management of service level requirements (SLRs) for all proposed new or changed services
- Development and management of appropriate operational level agreements (OLAs), ensuring alignment to SLAs
- Review of underpinning supplier contracts and agreements with supplier management, ensuring alignment with SLAs
- Proactive prevention of service failures, reduction of service risks and improvements in service quality, in conjunction with all other processes
- Reporting and management of services and review of SLA breaches and weaknesses
- Instigation and coordination of a service improvement plan (SIP) for the management, planning and implementation of all service and process improvements.

4.3   VALUE TO THE BUSINESS (SD 4.2, 4.2.3)

SLM negotiates, agrees and documents appropriate IT service targets with the business. It then monitors and produces reports on the service provider's ability to deliver the agreed level of service. Targets need to reflect business requirements so that the service delivered aligns with business requirements and meets customer expectations of service quality. An SLA provides assurance or warranty for the level of service quality to be delivered by the service provider.

SLM provides a consistent interface to the business for all service-related issues. Where targets are breached, SLM provides feedback on the cause and details the actions taken to prevent recurrence.

SLM provides a reliable communication channel and a trusted relationship with customer and business representatives.

4.4 POLICIES, PRINCIPLES AND BASIC CONCEPTS (SD 4.2.4, SD APPENDIX F)

SLM includes the planning, coordinating, drafting, agreeing, monitoring and reporting of SLAs, and the ongoing review of service achievements to ensure that the required and cost-justifiable service quality is maintained and gradually improved.

An SLA is a written agreement between an IT service provider and customer, defining the key service targets, warranty elements and responsibilities of both parties, detailing:

- Service description
- Scope of the agreement
- Service hours
- Service availability (warranty)
- Reliability
- Customer support
- Contact points and escalation
- Service performance and capacity (warranty)
- Change management
- Service continuity (warranty)
- Security (warranty)

- Charging (if applicable)
- Service reporting and reviewing.

SLM is responsible for ensuring that all targets and measures agreed in SLAs with the business are supported by underpinning OLAs or contracts with internal support units and external partners or suppliers.

An OLA is an agreement between an IT service provider and another part of the same organization that assists with service provision. An OLA contains targets that underpin those within an SLA to ensure that targets are not breached by failure of a supporting activity. An OLA typically comprises:

- Support service description
- Scope of the agreement
- Service hours
- Service targets
- Contact points and escalation
- Service desk and incident response times and responsibilities
- Problem response times and responsibilities
- Change management
- Release management
- Configuration management
- Information security management
- Availability management
- Service continuity management
- Capacity management
- Supplier management.

SLRs are customer requirements for an aspect of an IT service. They are based on business objectives and are used to negotiate agreed service level targets.

4.5   PROCESS ACTIVITIES, METHODS AND TECHNIQUES (SD 4.2.5, CSI 3.5)

Key activities within SLM include:

■ Design SLA frameworks
  Use the service catalogue to aid design of an SLA structure, ensuring all services and customers are covered to meet the organization's needs. Options include:
  – **Service-based SLA** An SLA covering all customers of that service. Multiple classes of service, e.g. gold, silver and bronze, can increase the effectiveness of service-based SLAs
  – **Customer-based SLA** An SLA with an individual customer group, covering all the services they use. Only one signatory is normally required

  A combination of the above structures might be appropriate, providing all services and customers are covered, with no overlap or duplication:

  – **Multi-level SLAs** For example, a three-layer structure: corporate level for all customers; customer level covering all services relevant to a particular business unit, regardless of the service being used; and service level relevant to a specific service for a specific customer group

■ Determine, negotiate, document and agree requirements for new or changed services via SLRs, and manage and review them through the service lifecycle into SLAs for operational services:
  – When the service catalogue has been produced and the SLA structure has been agreed, draft an initial SLR. Involve customers from the outset. Establish procedures for agreeing SLRs for new services being developed or procured

- SLRs need to be included in the service design criteria, forming part of the testing and trialling criteria as the service progresses through the stages of design and development or procurement
- Initial requirements may not be those ultimately agreed. Several iterations of negotiations may be required before an acceptable balance is struck between what is sought and what is achievable and affordable
- For new services being introduced into the live environment, undertake the planning and formalization of the support arrangements for the service. Define specific responsibilities and add to existing contracts and OLAs, or agree new ones
- Where appropriate, complete initial training, familiarization and knowledge transfer for the service desk and other support groups before live support is needed
- Negotiate the final SLA and the initial service level targets, using the draft agreement as a basis, with customers and service providers, to ensure these are achievable

- Monitor and measure service performance achievements of all operational services against targets within SLAs
  - Only include items in an SLA that can be effectively monitored and measured at a commonly agreed point. Inclusion of items that cannot be effectively monitored often leads to disputes and loss of faith in SLM
  - Existing monitoring capabilities need to be reviewed and upgraded as necessary, either before or in parallel to the drafting of SLAs, so that monitoring can assist with the validation of proposed targets

- Ensure any incident- or problem-handling targets included in SLAs are reflected in the service desk tools and that they are used for escalation and monitoring purposes
- Transaction response times can be difficult to monitor, so consider either including a statement in the SLA to indicate the acceptable time beyond which it is reported to the service desk, or implementing automated client or server response time monitoring
- Identify areas to improve levels of service as input into the SIP

■ Collate, measure and improve customer satisfaction
- Manage customers' expectations by setting appropriate targets in the first place, and manage their expectations going forward
- Where charges are being made for the services provided, this should modify customer demands. Otherwise use the support of senior business managers to ensure that excessive or unrealistic demands are not made
- Methods of monitoring customer perception include periodic questionnaires and customer surveys, feedback from service review meetings and post-implementation reviews, telephone perception surveys, user group or forum meetings and analysis of complaints and compliments
- All customer feedback needs to be acknowledged and comments incorporated in an action plan, perhaps a SIP. Review customer satisfaction measurements and analyse variations for actions to address

■ Review and revise underpinning agreements and service scope
  – Ensure that all targets in underpinning or 'back-to-back' agreements are aligned with, and support, targets agreed in the SLAs or OLAs. Where there are several layers of underpinning agreements, ensure the targets at each layer are aligned with, and support, the targets at the higher levels

■ Produce service reports
  – SLA reporting mechanisms, intervals and report formats must be defined and agreed with the customers and synchronized with the reviewing cycle. Circulate reports in advance of service level reviews, so that any queries or disagreements can be resolved ahead of the review meeting
  – Periodic reports detail performance against all SLA targets, together with details of any trends or specific actions being undertaken to improve service quality
  – Reports need to reflect the customer's perception of service quality. Information needs to be accurate and to have been analysed and collated into concise and comprehensive reports on service performance against agreed business targets
  – Reports can be time-consuming and effort-intensive, so identify specific reporting needs and automate reporting as far as possible

- Conduct service review and instigate improvements within an overall SIP
  - Periodic review meetings must be held on a regular basis with customers to review the service achievement in the last period and to preview any issues for the coming period. The frequency and format of service review meetings must be agreed with the customers. Regular intervals are recommended, for example monthly or quarterly
  - Action must be placed on the customer or provider, as appropriate, to improve weak areas where targets are not being met. Minute actions and review progress at the next meeting
  - For any breach of service level, determine the cause of service loss and what can be done to prevent any recurrence. It may be necessary to review, renegotiate and agree different service targets, including any underpinning agreement or OLA
  - Analyse the cost and impact of service breaches for input to and justification of SIP activities and actions. Report on the progress and success of the SIP

- Review and revise SLAs, service scope, OLAs, contracts, and any other underpinning agreements
  - All agreements and underpinning agreements must be reviewed periodically – at least annually – to ensure they remain current, comprehensive and aligned to business needs and strategy
  - Ensure the services covered and the targets for each are still relevant
  - Any changes need to be made under change management control

- Develop and document contacts and relationships with the business, customers and stakeholders. Develop trust and respect with the business, especially with the key business contacts
  - Confirm stakeholders, customers and key business managers and service users and assist with maintaining accurate information within the service portfolio and service catalogue
  - Ensure that the correct relationship processes are in place to achieve objectives and that they are subjected to continual improvement
  - Conduct and complete customer surveys, assist with the analysis of the completed surveys and ensure that actions are taken on the results
  - Act as an IT representative, organizing and attending user groups
  - Facilitate the development and negotiation of appropriate, achievable and realistic SLRs and SLAs between the business and IT
  - Ensure the business, customers and users understand their responsibilities and commitments to IT (i.e. IT dependencies)
- Develop, maintain and operate procedures for logging, actioning and resolving all complaints, and for logging and distributing compliments
- Log and manage all complaints and compliments
- Provide the appropriate management information to aid performance management and demonstrate service achievement
- Make available and maintain up-to-date SLM document templates and standards for SLAs, SLRs and OLAs to ensure all agreements are developed in a consistent manner; this will aid their subsequent use, operation and management.

The interfaces between the main activities are illustrated in Figure 4.1.

Figure 4.1 The service level management process

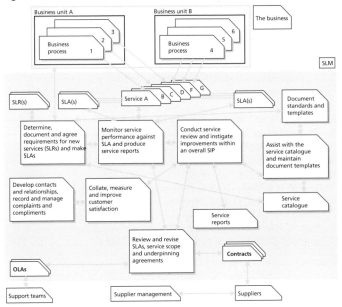

4.6   TRIGGERS, INPUTS, OUTPUTS AND INTERFACES (SD 4.2.5, 4.2.6)

Triggers include:

■ Changes in the strategy, policy or service portfolio, such as new or changed business requirements or new or changed services

- New or changed agreements, SLRs, SLAs, OLAs or contracts
- Service review meetings and actions and service breaches
- Periodic activities such as reviewing, reporting and customer satisfaction surveys, as well as compliments and complaints.

Inputs include:

- Business information from an organization's business strategy, plans and financial plans, and information on its current and future requirements
- Business impact analysis, providing information on the impact, priority, risk and number of users associated with each service
- Details of any agreed, new or changed business requirements
- Strategies, policies and constraints from service strategy, the service portfolio and service catalogue
- Customer and user feedback, complaints and compliments
- Other inputs: including advice, information and input from any of the other processes (e.g. incident management, change management, capacity management and availability management), together with the CMS, the existing SLAs, SLRs, OLAs and underpinning contracts, and past service reports on the quality of service delivered.

Outputs include:

- Service reports based on SLAs, OLAs and underpinning contracts
- SIPs
- The service quality plan, documenting and planning the overall improvement of service quality
- Document templates, format and content for SLAs, SLRs and OLAs, aligned with corporate standards
- SLAs, SLRs and OLAs

- Service review meeting minutes and actions, and SLA review and service scope review meeting minutes
- Revised contracts to align to changes to SLAs or new SLRs.

Key interfaces are:

- Business customers, stakeholders and business processes for determining SLRs, defining and agreeing SLAs, relationship management and managing customer satisfaction
- Service providers for definition, agreement and performance management for OLAs
- Change management providing feedback from post-implementation reviews following new or changed services and releases and managing change to agreements
- Configuration management for management of agreements as CIs
- Service improvement to support continual monitoring and improvement of levels of service.

4.7   METRICS AND MEASUREMENT (SD 4.2.7, 4.2.8)

Develop key performance indicators and metrics from the service, customer and business perspectives and include both subjective and objective measurements.

Manage the overall quality of IT service needed, both in the number and level of services provided and managed:

- Percentage reduction in SLA targets missed and threatened
- Percentage increase in customer perception and satisfaction of SLA achievements, via service reviews and customer satisfaction survey responses
- Percentage reduction in SLA breaches because of third-party support contracts (underpinning contracts)
- Percentage reduction in SLA breaches because of internal OLAs.

Deliver service as previously agreed at affordable costs:

- Number and percentage increase in fully documented SLAs in place
- Percentage increase in SLAs agreed against operational services
- Percentage reduction in the costs associated with service provision
- Frequency of service review meetings.

Manage business interface:

- Increased percentage of services covered by SLAs
- Increased percentage of SLA reviews completed on time
- Reduction in the percentage of outstanding SLAs for annual renegotiation
- Percentage increase in the coverage of OLAs and third-party contracts in place, whilst possibly reducing the actual number of agreements (consolidation and centralization)
- Reduction in the number and severity of SLA breaches
- Effective review and follow-up of all SLA, OLA and underpinning contract breaches.

SLM provides key information on all operational services, their expected targets and the service achievements and breaches for all operational services. It assists service catalogue management with the management of the service catalogue and also provides the information and trends on customer satisfaction, including complaints and compliments.

SLM is crucial in providing information on the quality of IT service provided to the customer, and information on the customer's expectation and perception of that quality of service. This information should be widely available to all areas of the service provider organization.

4.8   ROLES AND RESPONSIBILITIES (SD 6.4.6)

The service level manager has responsibility for ensuring that the aims of SLM are met, including responsibilities such as:

- Staying aware of changing business needs
- Ensuring the current and future service requirements of customers are identified, understood and documented in SLA and SLR documents
- Negotiating and agreeing levels of service to be delivered with the customer (either internal or external); formally documenting these levels of service in SLAs
- Negotiating and agreeing OLAs and agreements that underpin the SLAs with the customers of the service
- Assisting with the production and maintenance of an accurate service portfolio, service catalogue, application portfolio and the corresponding maintenance procedures
- Ensuring service reports are produced for each customer service and that SLA breaches are highlighted, investigated and actions taken to prevent recurrence
- Ensuring service performance reviews are scheduled, regularly carried out and documented, with agreed actions progressed and reported
- Reviewing service scope, SLAs, OLAs and other agreements on a regular basis
- Ensuring all changes are assessed for impact on service levels, including SLAs, OLAs and underpinning contracts, including attendance at Change Advisory Board meetings if appropriate
- Developing relationships and communication with stakeholders, customers and key users
- Defining, recording, agreeing, managing, escalating and communicating complaints
- Measuring, recording, analysing and improving customer satisfaction.

4.9 CHALLENGES, CRITICAL SUCCESS FACTORS AND RISKS (SD 4.2.9)

Challenges include:

- Identifying suitable customer representatives with whom to negotiate
- Lack of SLM experience: using draft SLAs and engaging with the more enthusiastic customer groups helps mitigate the risk of failure
- Ensuring all the appropriate and relevant customer requirements, at all levels, are identified and incorporated in SLAs, including targets that are realistic, achievable and affordable
- Getting the SLAs agreed and signed
- Underpinning the SLAs with OLAs and supplier contracts
- Publishing and communicating the agreed service levels to all stakeholders, including the service desk
- Establishing monitoring of service performance.

The main critical success factors for SLM include:

- Manage the overall quality of IT services required
- Deliver the service as previously agreed at an affordable cost
- Manage the interface with the business and users.

Risks associated with SLM include:

- A lack of accurate input, involvement and commitment from the business and customers
- Lack of tools and resources required to agree, document, monitor, report and review agreements and service levels
- Process becomes a bureaucratic, administrative process rather than an active and proactive process delivering measurable benefit to the business
- Bypassing the use of the SLM processes

- Business and customer measurements are too difficult to measure and improve, so they are not recorded
- Inappropriate business and customer contacts and relationships are developed
- High customer expectations and low perceptions.

5 Demand management

5.1 CONCEPTS (SS 5.5.1)

Demand management is a critical aspect of service management.

Poorly managed demand is a risk for service providers because of uncertainty in demand. Excess capacity can generate cost without creating the perceived value that provides a basis for cost recovery, although in reality it creates value through higher levels of service assurance. On the other hand, insufficient capacity can impact the quality of services and limit their growth.

Service management needs a tight coupling between demand and capacity, ideally synchronized, as unlike traditional products which may be created in a production cycle and then stored to satisfy a later sales cycle demand, IT services may only be used at the point when they are required.

Service level agreements, forecasting, planning, and coordination with the customer can reduce the uncertainty in demand but not eliminate it. Demand management techniques such as off-peak pricing, volume discounts and differentiated service levels can influence demand but not drive or create it.

Demand forecasts and business patterns can be used to align the capacity available to a service. Some types of capacity can be quickly adjusted as required: either increased to support demand or released when not in use.

5.2 PROCESS ACTIVITIES, METHODS AND TECHNIQUES (SS 5.1.2.2, 5.5.2, 5.5.3, 5.5.4, 7.4.3)

5.2.1 Activity-based demand management

An understanding of what creates demand patterns is key to IT service planners. Service demand is primarily driven by business processes, so PBA influence service demand patterns, as illustrated in Figure 5.1. Therefore, customer business patterns need to be identified, analysed and codified to provide input to capacity management, looking at these patterns in terms of demand for supporting services and underlying service assets.

Demand patterns can occur at multiple levels, so activity-based demand management can daisy-chain demand patterns to ensure business plans are synchronized with service management plans.

Figure 5.1 Business activity influences patterns of demand for services

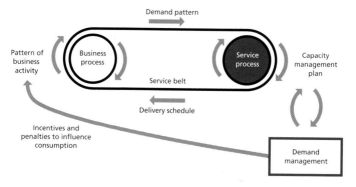

5.2.2 Business activity patterns and user profiles

Within business activities, customer assets (e.g. people, processes and applications) generate PBA. PBA define the dynamics of a business, including interactions with customers, suppliers, partners and other stakeholders. As PBA generate revenue, income and costs, they account for most business outcomes.

Attributes, including frequency, volume, location and duration, describe business activity, associated with requirements such as security, privacy, latency and tolerance for delays. PBA can change over time with changes and improvements in the business. Table 5.1 shows an excerpt from a sample PBA.

Table 5.1 Codifying patterns of business activity (example)

PBA No. 123	Activity levels			
	High	Medium	Low	N/A
Interacts with customers remotely (frequency)		X		
Processes sensitive information (privacy)				X
Network bandwidth requirements	X			
Data storage requirements (volume)	X			
Tolerance for delay in service response			X	

User profiles (UPs) are based on roles and responsibilities within organizations for people, and within functions and operations for processes and applications. Processes may be automated and so consume their own services. Therefore, processes and applications can have UPs.

Each UP can be associated with one or more predefined PBA, allowing aggregation and relationships for PBA to be made. UPs represent patterns that are persistent and correlated, ensuring a systematic approach to understanding and managing demand from customers. Table 5.2 shows an example of UPs matched with PBA.

PBA and UPs provide the basis for managing demand for service:

■ Enabling customers to better understand their business activities and view the activities as consumers of services and producers of demand
■ Providing service providers with information to sort and serve demand with appropriately matched services, service levels and service assets.

Sources of demand with similar workload characteristics can be identified and classified into distinct segments. Service designs, models and assets can then be specialized to serve a specific type of demand more effectively and efficiently.

This focus naturally leads to service assets that are optimized to meet the needs of groups of users with similar requirements. In this way customer satisfaction among those users will be increased.

PBA and UPs are managed as part of normal change control procedures.

Table 5.2 User profiles matched with business activity patterns (example)

User profile (UP)	Applicable pattern of business activity (PBA)	PBA code
Senior executive (UP1)	Moderate travel – domestic and overseas; highly sensitive information; zero latency on service requests; high need for technical assistance; need to be highly available to the business	45 21
Highly mobile executive (UP2)	Extensive travel – domestic and overseas; sensitive information; low latency on service requests; moderate need for technical assistance; high customer contact; need to be highly available to customers	33 06 17
Office-based staff (UP3)	Office-based administrative staff; low travel – domestic; medium latency on service requests; low need for technical assistance; full-featured desktop needs; moderate customer contact; high volume of paperwork; need to be highly productive during work hours	44 13 12

5.3   INTERFACES (SS 5.5.2)

Demand management can provide inputs to service management functions and processes including:

- **Service design** Optimizing designs to suit demand patterns
- **Service catalogue** Mapping demand patterns to appropriate services
- **Capacity management** Demand forecasts and PBA provide key inputs for capacity planning
- **Service portfolio management** Approving investments for additional capacity, new services, or changes to services
- **Service operation** Adjusting allocation of resources and scheduling
- **Service operation** Identifying opportunities to consolidate demand by grouping closely matching demand patterns
- **Financial management** Approving suitable incentives to influence demand.

6   Supplier management

6.1   PURPOSE/GOAL/OBJECTIVES (SD 4.7.1)

The purpose of supplier management is to obtain value for money from suppliers, ensuring they perform to the agreed or contracted targets, while conforming to all terms and conditions.

The goal of supplier management is to manage suppliers and the services they supply, to provide a seamless quality of IT service to the business, ensuring value for money is obtained.

The primary objectives of supplier management are to:

■ Obtain value for money from supplier and contracts
■ Ensure that underpinning supplier contracts and agreements are aligned to business needs, and support and align with agreed targets in SLRs and SLAs, in conjunction with SLM
■ Manage relationships with suppliers
■ Manage supplier performance
■ Negotiate and agree contracts with suppliers and manage them through their lifecycle
■ Maintain a supplier policy and a supporting supplier and contract database (SCD).

It is essential that supplier management processes and planning are involved in all stages of the service lifecycle.

6.2   SCOPE (SD 4.7.2)

Supplier management includes the management of all suppliers and contracts needed to support the provision of IT services to the business. The process is adapted according to the importance of the supplier and/or contract and the potential business impact on the provision of services.

Supplier management includes:

- Implementation and enforcement of the supplier policy
- Maintenance of an SCD
- Supplier and contract categorization and risk assessment
- Supplier and contract evaluation and selection
- Development, negotiation and agreement of contracts
- Contract review, renewal and termination
- Management of suppliers and supplier performance
- Agreement and implementation of service and supplier improvement plans
- Maintenance of standard contracts, terms and conditions
- Management of contractual dispute resolution
- Management of subcontracted suppliers.

IT supplier management may have to comply with organizational or corporate standards, guidelines and requirements, e.g. corporate legal, finance or purchasing.

Each supplier needs to be owned by a nominated person within the organization. Roles need to be established for a supplier management process owner and a contracts manager.

6.3 VALUE TO THE BUSINESS (SD 4.7.3)

Supplier management provides value to the business by ensuring:

- Value for money from suppliers and contracts
- That all targets in underpinning supplier contracts and agreements are aligned to business needs and agreed targets within SLAs
- Delivery to the business of end-to-end, seamless, high-quality IT services that are aligned to the business's expectation.

6.4 POLICIES, PRINCIPLES AND BASIC CONCEPTS (SD 4.7.4)

A supplier strategy and policy drives all supplier management activities. An SCD, with clearly defined supplier management roles and responsibilities, achieves consistency and effectiveness in the implementation of the policy. The SCD forms an integrated element of a comprehensive CMS or service knowledge management system, containing a complete set of reference information for all supplier management procedures and activities.

6.5 PROCESS ACTIVITIES, METHODS AND TECHNIQUES (SD 4.7.5)

For external service providers, or suppliers, a formal contract with defined, agreed and documented responsibilities and targets needs to be established and managed, from the identification of the business need to the operation and cessation of the contract.

Identification of business need and preparation of the business case:

- Produce a statement of requirements and/or invitation to tender
- Ensure conformance to strategy/policy
- Prepare the initial business case, including options (internal and external), costs, timescales, targets, benefits and risk assessment.

Evaluation and procurement of new contracts and suppliers:

- Determine the approach to sourcing, e.g. single provider, multi-sourced or partnering. Partnering relationships are characterized by strategic alignment, integration, information flow, openness, collective responsibility, and shared risk and reward

- Establish the evaluation criteria, e.g. the importance and impact of service to the business, supplier capability (both personnel and organization), quality, risks and cost
- Evaluate alternative supplier options and select supplier(s)
- Negotiate contracts, targets and the terms and conditions, including service description and standards, workload ranges, management information to be reported, responsibilities and dependencies
- Agree and award the contract: formal contracts are appropriate for external supplier agreements where an enforceable commitment is required. For internal service providers an underpinning agreement such as an OLA formalizes the arrangement via SLM.

Supplier and contract categorization:

- Assessment or reassessment of the supplier and contract, e.g. based on risk and impact of using a supplier against the value and importance of the supplied service to the business
- Categorization of the supplier:
  - Categorize suppliers as 'strategic', 'tactical', 'operational' or 'commodity' to ensure that appropriate levels of time and effort are spent managing the supplier relationship
  - Categorization can be based on contract price, business value (contribution to the business value chain), or level of service customization (increasing business value but also dependencies, risk and cost)
  - Business services may depend on a mix of internal and external suppliers of different categorizations. Supply chain analysis can be used to identify the mapping between business services and suppliers. Supply chain management can then ensure clarity of requirements for each supplier to ensure overall business service levels are achieved

- Update the SCD, containing supplier details, service and product summaries, ordering details and contract details.

Establish new suppliers and contracts:

- Set up the supplier service and contract, within the SCD and any other associated corporate systems via change management
- Establish risk management activities for the supplier, e.g. operational risk assessments and/or business impact analysis. This needs to be ongoing, reflecting changes to business needs, the contract or the operational environment
- Undertake transition of service
- Establish contacts, relationships and reviews, and add them to the SCD.

Manage supplier and contract performance:

- Ensure that a single, nominated individual is accountable for all aspects for each supplier relationship
- Management and control of the operation and delivery of the service or products, including integrated processes and systems, and escalation
- Service and supplier performance reports and reviews – these should be more frequent and more extensive for the more important suppliers, and include any improvement activities, required or in progress
- Governance of the supplier, contracts and the relationship (communication, risks, changes, failures, improvements, contacts, interfaces)
- Control major service improvements through SIPs
- Ongoing maintenance of the SCD
- Service, service scope and contract reviews, at least annually, considering overall performance, original and current business needs, delivery of value for money, business satisfaction and benefits realization.

Contract renewal and/or termination:

- Contract review to ensure that the contract continues to meet business needs. Consider aspects such as contract delivery and governance, relevance to future needs, changes required, performance and pricing against benchmarks or market assessments
- Assess the impact, risks, costs (including exit costs), legal implications and benefits for any proposed change of supplier
- Renegotiate and renew or terminate and/or transfer contract and service.

The business, IT, finance, purchasing and procurement need to work together to ensure that all stages of the contract lifecycle are managed effectively.

Vary the above based on the type, size and category of supplier and contract.

6.6 TRIGGERS, INPUTS, OUTPUTS AND INTERFACES (SD 4.7.6)

Triggers include:

- New or changed business and IT strategies, policies or plans
- New or changed business needs, services or requirements within agreements, e.g. SLAs
- Periodic activities such as reviewing, revising or reporting, including review and revision of supplier management policies, reports and plans
- Requests from other areas, particularly SLM and security management, for assistance with supplier issues
- Requirements for new contracts, contract renewal or contract termination
- Recategorization of suppliers and/or contracts.

Inputs include:

- Business information: business strategy and plans, financial plans, and current and future requirements
- Supplier and contracts strategy: sourcing policy and types of suppliers and contracts used
- Supplier plans and strategies: supplier business plans and strategies, technology developments and plans, current financial status and projected business viability
- Supplier contracts, agreements and targets, and performance information
- IT strategy, plans and current budgets
- Performance issues: incidents and problems relating to poor contract or supplier performance
- Financial information: the cost of supplier services, the cost of contracts and the resultant business benefit, financial plans and budgets, plus the costs of service and supplier failure
- Service information: details of services in the service portfolio and service catalogue, service level targets within SLAs and SLRs, and the actual service performance from service reports, reviews and breaches. Also customer satisfaction data on service quality
- CMS: relationships between the business, the services, the supporting services and the technology.

Outputs include:

- SCD: this holds the information needed by all subprocesses within supplier management
- Supplier and contract performance information and reports
- Supplier and contract review meeting minutes
- Supplier SIPs
- Supplier survey reports.

Key interfaces include:

- **IT service continuity management** Managing continuity service suppliers
- **SLM** Ensuring that targets, requirements and responsibilities support all SLR and SLA targets, and investigating SLR or SLA breaches caused by poor supplier performance
- **Information security management (ISM)** Managing supplier access to services and systems, and their conformance to ISM policies and requirements
- **Financial management** Providing adequate funds for supplier management requirements and contracts, plus guidance on purchasing and procurement
- **Service portfolio management** Ensuring that all supporting services are accurately reflected in the service portfolio.

6.7 METRICS AND MEASUREMENT (SD 4.7.7)

Metrics to assess the effectiveness and efficiency of the supplier management need to be considered from the service, customer and business perspectives; for example:

- Business protection against poor supplier performance or disruption:
  - Increase in the number of suppliers meeting contracted targets
  - Reduction in the number of breaches of contracted targets
- Supporting services and targets align with business needs and targets:
  - Increase in the number of service and contractual reviews held with suppliers
  - Increase in the number of supplier and contractual targets aligned with SLR and SLA targets

- Availability of services not compromised by supplier performance:
  - Reduction in the number of service breaches caused by suppliers
  - Reduction in the number of potential service breaches caused by suppliers
- Ownership and awareness of supplier and contractual issues:
  - Increase in the number of suppliers with nominated supplier managers
  - Increase in the number of contracts with nominated contract managers.

6.8 ROLES AND RESPONSIBILITIES (SD 6.4.11)

The key responsibility of the supplier manager is to ensure that the aims of supplier management are met, including key tasks such as:

- Supporting the development and review of SLAs, contracts and agreements for suppliers, ensuring they are aligned with those of the business
- Ensuring that value for money is obtained from all IT suppliers and contracts
- Maintaining and reviewing an SCD
- Reviewing and risk analysis of all suppliers and contracts on a regular basis
- Ensuring that all supporting services are scoped and documented and that interfaces and dependencies between suppliers, supporting services and supplier processes are agreed and documented
- Performing contract or SLA reviews at least annually, and ensuring that all contracts are consistent with organizational requirements and standard terms and conditions wherever possible

- Updating contracts or SLAs when required, ensuring that the change management process is followed
- Maintaining processes for existing contracts and handling contractual disputes
- Monitoring, reporting and regularly reviewing supplier performance against targets, identifying improvement actions as appropriate and ensuring these actions are implemented
- Ensuring changes are assessed for their impact on suppliers, supporting services and contracts and attending Change Advisory Board (CAB) meetings when appropriate
- Coordinating and supporting IT supplier and contract managers, ensuring that each supplier and contract has a nominated owner within the service provider organization.

6.9 CHALLENGES, CRITICAL SUCCESS FACTORS AND RISKS (SD 4.7.9)

Challenges include:

- Continually changing business and IT needs and managing significant change in parallel with delivering existing service
- Working with an imposed non-ideal contract, e.g. one with poor targets or terms and conditions
- Insufficient expertise retained within the organization or personality conflicts
- Being tied into long-term contracts, with no possibility of improvement, which have punitive penalty charges for early exit
- Supplier dependencies on the organization in fulfilling the service delivery (e.g. for a data feed) can lead to issues over accountability for poor service performance
- Disputes over charges

■ Communication – not interacting often enough or quickly enough or not focusing on the right issues.

Critical success factors include:

■ Business protection from poor supplier performance or disruption
■ Supporting services and their targets align with business needs and targets
■ Availability of services is not compromised by supplier performance
■ Clear ownership and awareness of supplier and contractual issues.

Major risks include:

■ Lack of commitment from the business and senior management
■ Legacy of badly written and agreed contracts that do not underpin or support business needs or SLR/SLA targets
■ Suppliers agree to targets and service levels within contracts that are impossible to meet, or suppliers fail or are incapable of meeting the terms and conditions of the contract
■ Supplier's personnel or organizational culture is not aligned to that of the service provider or the business
■ Suppliers are not cooperative or willing to participate in the supplier management process
■ Suppliers are taken over and relationships, personnel and contracts are changed
■ Poor corporate financial processes, such as procurement and purchasing, do not support good supplier management.

7 Financial management

7.1 PURPOSE/GOAL/OBJECTIVES (SS 5.1, 5.1.1)

Financial management quantifies, in clear financial terms, the value of IT services and the underpinning service assets, and the qualification of operational forecasts. It helps service providers to understand and control the factors that influence supply and demand and to deliver services as cost-effectively as possible, whilst maximizing the visibility of the related cost structure.

Financial management is applicable to all three service provider types: internal service provider, shared service unit and external service provider.

IT service providers use financial management to support the development and execution of their service strategy, achieving:

- Enhanced decision making
- Speed of change
- Service portfolio management
- Financial compliance and control
- Operational control
- Value capture and creation.

Financial management generates meaningful critical performance data to steer strategic decisions, service design and tactical operational decisions.

7.2 SCOPE (SS 5.1.2)

The financial management data used by an IT organization may reside in, and be owned by, the accounting and finance domain, but responsibility for generating and utilizing it extends to other areas, including operations, project management, application development and business units. Financial management aggregates data inputs from across the enterprise and assists in generating and disseminating information as an output to feed critical decisions and activities.

7.3   VALUE TO THE BUSINESS (SS 5.1, 5.1.1)

The business benefits from the operational visibility, insights and improved decision making enabled by good financial management and financial data.

Financial management provides a common language between the business and IT. It enables service valuation, which is used to help the business and the IT service provider agree on the value of the IT service, to take place. Service valuation can also transform the interaction between IT and the business, and the way the business plans for and consumes IT services. A powerful benefit is financial management's provision of cost transparency for services in a way that can be clearly understood by the business and rolled into planning processes for demand modelling and funding.

7.4   POLICIES, PRINCIPLES AND BASIC CONCEPTS

7.4.1   Service valuation (SS 5.1.2.1)

Service valuation is a measure of the cost of delivering an IT service, or service component, and its value to the business. It enables the business and IT service provider to agree on the monetary value of the IT service by identifying the cost baseline for a service and then quantifying the perceived value added by a provider's service assets in order to determine the service value.

It is important to produce a value for services that the business perceives as fair, meets its needs and can be used to improve management of demand and consumption behaviours.

Service valuation concepts:

- **Provisioning value** The cost to the IT service provider of delivering a specific service to a customer. This includes costs associated with hardware and software, annual maintenance fees, personnel, facilities and power consumption, compliance, taxes and interest charges. The sum of the actual costs represents the baselines from which the minimum value of a service is calculated
- **Service value potential** The value-added component based on the customer's perception of value from the service or expected marginal utility and warranty from using the service, as compared to using the customer's own assets. Techniques such as service-oriented accounting are used to associate specific monetary values to each perceived value-added component of the service. The sum of these perceived values is the service value potential, which is added to the provisioning value to calculate the ultimate value of the service.

7.4.2 Planning confidence (SS 5.1.2.5)

Planning provides, in financial terms, the expected future demand for IT services. Financial management planning focuses on demand and supply variances resulting from business strategy, capacity inputs and forecasting.

Planning categories include:

- **Operating and capital (general and fixed asset ledgers)** Typically common and standardized processes, but it is important to notify other business areas of any expected changes in the funding of IT services

- **Demand (need and use of IT services)** Quantifying funding variations from changes in service demand using service-oriented financial information
- **Regulatory and environmental (compliance)** Triggered from within the business, but proper financial inputs to the related services value, whether cost-based or value-based, need to be applied.

Confidence in financial management planning data is important because of the critical role it plays in achieving the objectives of financial management, and the potential impact of incorrect data undermining decision making. It is key to ensure that the confidence level of planning data and information is high.

7.4.3 Service investment analysis (SS 5.1.2.6)

The objective of service investment analysis is to derive a value indication for the total lifecycle of a service based on the value received, and the costs incurred during the lifecycle of the service.

Assumptions about the service are a key component of analysing investments. The granularity of the assumptions can have significant impact on the outcome of the analysis. It is better to have an exhaustive list of assumptions than a limited number of high-level ones, to determine the most realistic and accurate view of the investment being made.

7.4.4 Accounting (SS 5.1.2.7)

Financial management accounting differs from traditional accounting as extra categories and characteristics are required to identify and track service-oriented items.

The functions and accounting characteristics required are:

- **Service recording** Allocating a cost entry to the appropriate service
- **Cost types** High-level expenses categories, e.g. hardware, software, labour and administration, to support reporting and analysing of demand and service usage, in financial terms
- **Cost classifications** For services, these designate the end purpose of the cost, for example:
  - Capital or operational
  - Direct or indirect: direct costs are charged directly to a service, whereas indirect or 'shared' costs are allocated across multiple services
  - Fixed or variable: based on contractual commitments of time or price
  - Cost units: the identified unit of consumption for a service or service asset.

7.4.5 Chargeback (SS 5.1.4.2)

A 'chargeback' model for IT provides accountability and visibility where required, e.g. for a self-funding IT organization.

Visibility is achieved by identification of service portfolios and catalogues, valuing the IT services, and applying these values to demand or consumption models.

Accountability relates to:

- IT's ability to deliver the expected services as agreed with the business
- The business's fulfilment of its obligations in funding these services.

When charging, the operating model needs to be considered; otherwise the required levels of accountability and visibility may not be delivered.

Charging encourages behavioural changes influencing demand for IT services. It must add value to the business, be in business terms, and be perceived as fair.

Chargeback models vary, based on their simplicity and the business's ability to understand them, such as:

- **Notional charging** Addresses whether a journal entry is made to the corporate financial systems
- **Tiered subscription** Involves offering different levels of warranty and/or utility for a service, each for a different price, e.g. gold, silver and bronze levels of service
- **Metered usage** Combines demand modelling with utility computing capabilities to provide real-time usage data which is used to charge the customer based on various service increments that have been agreed, e.g. hours, days or weeks
- **Direct plus** Charges based on costs that can be directly attributed to a service with some percentage of indirect costs shared amongst all
- **Fixed or user cost** Divides the total cost by an agreed denominator such as number of users. A simplistic model, but it has little impact on customer behaviour, or identification of true service demand or consumption.

7.4.6   Return on investment (SS 5.2 [to 5.2.2.1], 5.2.3 [to 5.2.3.1])

Return on investment (ROI) is a concept for quantifying the value of an investment and, at its simplest, is net profit of an investment divided by the net worth of the asset. In service management, it is used as a measure of the ability to use assets to generate additional value.

Organizations often apply the ROI to the adoption of service management. However, while a service can be justified through specific business imperatives, the financial return for aspects of service management can be difficult to identify.

A key challenge when trying to fund ITIL projects is identifying a specific business imperative that depends on service management. Three techniques to support this are:

■ **Business case** A means to identify business imperatives that depend on service management
■ **Pre-programme ROI** Techniques for quantitatively analysing an investment in service management
■ **Post-programme ROI** Techniques for retroactively analysing an investment in service management.

7.4.6.1 Business case

A business case is a decision support and planning tool. Its structure varies but should always include detailed analysis, typically financial, of business impact or benefits. Business impact is linked to business objectives, e.g. the reason for considering a service management initiative.

A typical business case structure includes:

■ **Introduction** Outlines the business objectives addressed by the service
■ **Methods and assumptions** Defines the boundaries of the business case, e.g. time period, whose costs and whose benefits
■ **Business impacts** Financial and non-financial business case results
■ **Risks and contingencies** Considers the probability that alternative results will emerge
■ **Recommendations** Specific recommended actions.

While most of a business case argument relies on cost analysis, for a service management initiative there are more than just financial considerations. Non-financial business impacts need to be linked to business objectives to show value. This does not need to be a one-to-one relationship between business impact and business objective.

Table 7.1 illustrates some common business objectives.

Linking business impacts to business objectives delivers a more compelling business case and enables both financial and non-financial analysis to occur.

7.4.6.2   Pre-programme return on investment

Capital budgeting is the commitment of funds now in order to receive a return in the future in the form of additional cash inflows or reduced cash outflows. Service management initiatives may sometimes require capital budgeting.

There are two categories of capital budgeting decisions:

- **Screening and preference decisions** Based on whether a proposed service management initiative passes a predetermined criterion, e.g. minimum return
- **Preference decisions** Choosing from several competing alternatives, e.g. different internal initiatives.

7.4.6.3   Post-programme return on investment

Many service management initiatives are implemented without a business case or plan. However, without clearly defined financial objectives, the added value brought about by service management cannot be measured and without proof of value, further investments may not be supported. So for any service management initiative without prior ROI analysis, an analysis should be conducted at an appropriate time afterwards.

Table 7.1 Common business objectives

Operational	Financial	Strategic	Industry
Shorten development time	Improve return on assets	Establish or enhance strategic positioning	Increase market share
Increase productivity	Avoid costs	Introduce competitive products	Improve market position
Increase capacity	Increase discretionary spending as a percentage of budget	Improve professionalism of organization	Increase repeat business
Increase reliability	Decrease non-discretionary spending	Improve customer satisfaction	Take market leadership
Minimize risks	Increase revenues	Provide better quality	Recognized as a producer of reliable or quality products or services
Improve resource utilization	Increase margins	Provide customized offerings	Recognized as low-price leader
Improve efficiencies	Keep spending to within budget	Introduce new products or services	Recognized as compliant with industry standards

Figure 7.1 illustrates the basic model for ROI calculation for service management.

Figure 7.1 Post-programme ROI approach

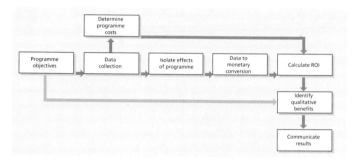

Programme objectives need to be clear, determining the depth and scope of the ROI analysis. Objectives can include:

- Deliver consistent and repeatable service
- Lower the overall total cost of ownership
- Improve quality of service
- Implement industry-wide best practices
- Provide an overall structure and process
- Facilitate the use of common concepts and terminology.

7.5 PROCESS ACTIVITIES, METHODS AND TECHNIQUES (SS 5.1.3)

7.5.1 Service valuation

During service valuation, there are some common issues that all IT centres need to address:

■ **Direct versus indirect costs** Costs that are either directly attributable to a specific service or indirect costs that are shared across multiple services. Approach this issue logically, based on the data available and the level of effort required to maintain. For indirect costs, once the depth and breadth of these components are identified, rules or policy to guide how costs are to be spread among multiple services may be required

■ **Labour costs** Similar to that of 'direct versus indirect costs', compounded by the complexity and accuracy of time tracking systems. If the allocation of these costs across services is not available, then rules and assumptions must be created for allocation of these costs

■ **Variable cost elements** Expenditures that are not fixed, but may vary, e.g. by the number of users. Determine the approach based on the identification of those services that cause increases in variability, as this can impact price sensitivity. Pricing variability over time can require rules to allow for predictability, requiring the tracking of specific consumption over time to establish ranges. Predictability can be addressed through:
  – **Tiers** Identifying price breaks where plateaus occur
  – **Maximum cost** Cost of service based on the maximum level of variability
  – **Average cost** Cost of the service based on historical averaging of the variability

■ **Translation from cost account data to service value** Only possible once costs are attributed to services rather than, or in addition to, traditional cost accounts.

Detailed service-oriented costs are captured to establish the underlying cost baseline for the service (i.e. provisioning value). The value-added component (i.e. service value potential) is derived based on the value of any anticipated marginal enhancement to the utility and warranty of a customer's existing service assets. This enables the total potential value of the service to be determined.

Identify the variable cost drivers and range of variability for a service to determine any additional amount to be added to the calculation of potential service value to allow for absorption of consumption variability.

Pricing the perceived value portion of a service involves resolving differences between historical costs, the perceived value added and planned demand variances.

7.5.2 Service provisioning models and analysis

- **Managed services provisioning model** A business unit requiring a service funds the service provision itself and the service provider calculates the service costs in terms of development, infrastructure, human resources, etc. so that the business and the service provider can plan for funding
- **Shared services model** Targets the provisioning of multiple services to one or more business units through use of shared infrastructure and resources, typically giving significant cost savings through the increased utilization of existing resources
- **Utility-based provisioning model** Providing services on a utilization basis, dependent on how much, how often, and at what times the customer needs them, maximizing the number of services being provisioned using the same resources found in the shared services model. This is the most cost-effective model, achieving cost savings through leveraging knowledge of technology architectures and customer needs to derive a combination of service and architecture that enables the maximum utilization of existing resources

- **On-shore, off-shore or near-shore** Many service elements (covered in the *Service Strategy*, *Service Design*, *Service Transition* and *Service Operation* publications) need to be combined to determine the right mix of on-shore, near-shore and off-shore service provisioning for any specific company at a specific time. However, if an organization does not understand its core service cost components and variable cost dynamics, it can be difficult to make logical and fact-based decisions regarding outsourcing models
- **Service provisioning cost analysis** The activity of statistically ranking the various forms of provisioning (and often providers) to determine the most beneficial model.

7.5.3 Funding model alternatives

Funding addresses the financial impacts from changes to current and future demand for IT services and how IT will retain the funds for ongoing operations.

Some traditional models for the funding of IT services are:

- **Rolling plan funding** As one cycle completes, another cycle of funding is added, encouraging a constant cycle of funding
- **Trigger-based plans** When an identified critical trigger occurs it sets off planning for a particular event
- **Zero-based funding** Sufficient funding only to cover the actual cost of the IT organization or service, bringing the financial balance back to zero until another funding cycle.

The chosen model should consider and be appropriate for the business culture and expectations.

7.5.4   Business impact analysis

Business impact analysis (BIA) identifies an organization's most critical business services through analysis of outage severity translated into a financial value, combined with operational risk. It is a useful tool for identifying the cost of service outage and the relative worth of a service:

■ Cost of service outage is a financial value which reflects the value of lost productivity and revenue over a specific period of time

■ Worth of a service, relative to other services in a portfolio, is derived from financial characteristics and aspects such as the ability to complete work or communicate with clients (which may not be directly related to revenue generation).

Both of these can be identified through BIA.

To generate a BIA, high-level activities include:

■ Arrange for business and IT resources to work together on the analysis

■ Identify the potential services for designation as critical, secondary and tertiary

■ Identify the core elements for use in assessing risk and impact, e.g. lost sales revenue, lost productivity or lost opportunity

■ Weight the identified elements of risk and impact with the business

■ Score the services against the weighted elements and total scores

■ Create a list of services in order of risk profile, i.e. total scores

■ Determine a standard time period against which service outages are translated into cost (e.g. by minute, hour or day)

■ Calculate the financial impact of each service using agreed methods, formulas and assumptions

- Generate a list of services in order of financial impact
- Use the risk and financial impact data to chart the highest-risk applications that also carry the greatest financial impact.

7.6   DESIGN AND IMPLEMENT A FINANCIAL MANAGEMENT PROCESS (SS 5.1.4.3)

The following is a sample checklist of recommended implementation steps.

7.6.1   Track 1 – Plan

- Address critical questions about the business and IT culture prior to implementing financial management, e.g. organizational considerations
- Assess the corporate culture, as geographical considerations will have additional regulatory and compliance considerations
- Identify all internal and external contacts that provide or receive IT financial information
- Be clear about IT and business expectations, e.g. deliverables or a chargeback system
- Determine the existing systems with which financial management will receive and contribute data
- Determine the funding or operating model to be used
- Assign responsibilities for the deliverables and outline the activities to be performed
- Prepare the organization chart based on the activities to be performed, the size of the data to be managed, and the tools available
- Prepare a policy and operating procedures list.

7.6.2   Track 2 – Analyse

■ Gather in-depth details around the planning and funding items previously identified, including analysis of the data for service valuation and demand modelling

■ Ensure all processes and information required to produce the expected deliverables are accounted for as part of financial management responsibilities

■ Prepare for creating new valuation and funding documents by familiarization with current expenses. To properly report and account for service costs, centralization of IT expenditures is a prerequisite

■ Undertake service valuation, reporting on the valuation pricing of service assets. If the operating model allows for the addition of value-added pricing, add that value to each service to calculate the total price for an IT service

■ Where financial management dependent processes are not available, adjust the plans for implementation for this to be addressed.

7.6.3   Track 3 – Design

■ Work with key contributors and supporters during this track, designing data inputs and translations, reports, methodologies and models

■ Identify all processes in place within IT and design clear 'hooks' into financial management

■ Prepare and test valuation models for appropriateness to the business environment

■ Finalize the accounting processes and procedures based on the knowledge obtained from the initial accounting of IT expenditures, identifying which reports are relevant to the operating model and business environment

■ Create the chosen chargeback methodology

- Complete the design of financial management policies and procedures
- Prepare the job descriptions and fill the required roles.

7.6.4   Track 4 – Implement

- **Activation of planned processes** Initial input is via corporate financial systems and change management processes; key hooks to data translation are via:
    - **Accounting** The first process that receives financial data for translation
    - **Change and demand management** First awareness of anticipated changes to IT.

7.6.5   Track 5 – Measure

- Provide measures of success on financial trends within funding, valuing and accounting
- Audit for any credibility gap between the value received and price paid as soon as possible. Audits need to be performed regularly as financial management owns the data that is translated to create financial data.

8 Business relationship manager

8.1 ROLE (SS 4.1.3, 5.5.4.5)

Business relationship management is responsible for gaining insight into the customer's business. Having good knowledge of customer outcomes is essential to developing a strong business relationship with customers, including:

- Managing personal relationships with business managers
- Providing input to service portfolio management
- Ensuring that the IT service provider is satisfying the business needs of the customers.

The business relationship manager (BRM) role is responsible for maintaining the relationship with one or more customers and is often combined with the service level manager role. BRMs:

- Are 'customer-focused' and manage opportunities through a customer portfolio
- May be known as account managers, business representatives or sales managers
- Identify the most suitable combination of lines of service (LOS) and service level packages (SLPs) for every customer outcome they are concerned with
- Relate customer outcomes to the supporting user profiles (UPs). Each UP is then matched to the appropriate SLP to create a customized service offering for every customer outcome using models such as the Kano Model
- Represent customers and work closely with product managers to ensure that the service catalogue has the right mix of LOS and SLPs to fulfil the customer's needs.

Internal IT service providers need this role to develop and be responsive to their internal market.

9 Technology and implementation

9.1 GENERIC REQUIREMENTS FOR ITSM TECHNOLOGY (SD 7.1)

There are many tools and techniques that can be used to assist with the design of services. They enable:

- Hardware design
- Software design
- Environmental design
- Process design
- Data design.

The tools and techniques are useful in:

- Speeding up the design process
- Ensuring standards are followed
- Prototyping, modelling and simulation
- Enabling 'what if?' analysis
- Enabling interfaces and dependencies to be checked
- Validating designs before development starts.

Developing service designs can be simplified by the use of tools that provide graphical views of the service and its constituent components. They can also be linked to auto-discovery tools to make the capture and maintenance of the relationships between all of the service components more efficient and accurate.

There is an opportunity to extend the use of these tools into day-to-day operation and, by linking to financial information, metrics and key performance indicators, they can be used to monitor and manage the service through all stages of its lifecycle.

The following generic activities are required to implement such an approach:

- Establish the generic lifecycle for IT assets (requirements, design and develop, build, test, deploy, operate and optimize, dispose) and define the principal processes, policies, activities and technologies within each stage of the lifecycle for each type of asset
- Formalize the relationships between different types of IT asset, and the relationship between IT asset acquisition and management and other IT disciplines
- Define all roles and responsibilities involved in IT asset activities
- Establish measures for understanding the (total) cost of ownership of an IT service
- Establish policies for the re-use of IT assets across services, e.g. at the corporate level
- Define a strategy for the acquisition and management of IT assets, including how it aligns with other IT and business strategies.

Additional activities should be carried out for specific asset types; for example:

- Applications
- Data or information
- IT infrastructure and environmental
- Skills (people, competencies)
- Interfaces and dependencies.

9.2 EVALUATION CRITERIA FOR TECHNOLOGY AND TOOLS (SD 7.2)

The following generic criteria apply to selection of any service management tool:

- Data handling, integration, import, export and conversion
- Data backup, control and security
- Ability to integrate multi-vendor components, now and into the future
- Conformity to international open standards
- Usability, scalability and flexibility of implementation and usage
- Support options provided by the vendor, and credibility of the vendor and tool
- The platform the tool will run on and how this fits the IT strategy
- Training and other requirements for customizing, deploying and using the tool
- Initial costs and ongoing costs.

It is generally best to select a fully integrated tool, but this must support the processes used by the organization, and extensive tool customization should be avoided.

Consideration should also be given to the organization's exact requirements. These should be documented in a statement of requirements. Tool requirements should be categorized using MoSCoW analysis:

- **M** – MUST have this
- **S** – SHOULD have this if at all possible
- **C** – COULD have this if it does not affect anything else
- **W** – WON'T have this, but WOULD like in the future.

Each proposed tool can be evaluated against these criteria to ensure the most appropriate tool is selected.

9.3 GOOD PRACTICES FOR PROCESS IMPLEMENTATION

9.3.1 Service level requirements (SD 8.2)

As part of service level management, the SLRs for all services will be ascertained and the ability to deliver against these requirements will be assessed and finally agreed in a formal SLA. For new services, the requirements must be ascertained at the start of the development process, not after completion. Building the service with SLRs uppermost in mind is essential from a service design perspective.

9.3.2 Risks to the services and processes (SD 8.3)

When implementing the service design and ITSM processes, usual business practices must not be adversely affected. This aspect must be considered during the production and selection of the preferred solution to ensure that disruption to operational services is minimized. This assessment of risk should then be considered in detail in the service transition activities as part of the implementation process.

9.3.3 Implementing service design (SD 8.4)

The process, policy and architecture for the design of IT services will need to be documented and utilized to ensure that appropriate innovative IT services can be designed and implemented to meet current and future agreed business requirements.

What is ultimately required is a single, integrated set of processes, providing management and control of a set of IT services throughout their entire lifecycle.

Areas of greatest need should be addressed first. A detailed assessment needs to be undertaken to ascertain the strengths and weaknesses of IT service provision.

It may be that 'quick wins' need to be implemented in the short term to improve the current situation but, if quick wins are implemented, it is important that they are not done at the expense of the long-term objectives.

Implementation priorities should be set against the goals of a SIP. For example, if availability of IT services is a critical issue, focus on those processes aimed at maximizing availability (e.g. incident management, problem management, change management and availability management).

Establish a formal process and method for implementation and improvement of service design, with the appropriate governance in place. This formal process should be based around the six-stage continual service improvement model, as shown in Figure 9.1.

- **Step one** Understand the vision by ascertaining the high-level business objectives. The 'vision-setting' should set and align business and IT strategies
- **Step two** Assess the current situation to identify strengths that can be built on and weaknesses that need to be addressed. Perform an analysis of the current position in terms of the business, organization, people and process
- **Step three** Develop the principles defined in the vision-setting and agree the priorities for improvement
- **Step four** Detail the SIP to achieve higher-quality service provision

Figure 9.1 The continual service improvement model

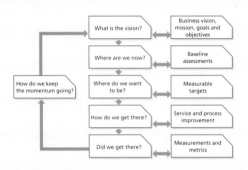

- **Step five** Put in place measurements and metrics to show that the milestones have been achieved and that the business objectives and business priorities have been met
- **Step six** Ensure that the momentum for quality improvement is maintained.

The following are key elements for successful alignment of IT with business objectives:

- Vision and leadership in setting and maintaining strategic direction, clear goals, and measurement of goal realization in terms of strategic direction
- Acceptance of innovation and new ways of working

- Thorough understanding of the business, its stakeholders and its environment
- IT staff understanding the needs of the business
- The business understanding the potential of IT
- Information and communication available and accessible to everyone who needs it
- Separately allocated time to become familiar with the material
- Continuous tracking of technologies to identify opportunities for the business.

9.4 CHALLENGES, CRITICAL SUCCESS FACTORS AND RISKS RELATING TO IMPLEMENTING PRACTICES AND PROCESSES (ST 9.1–9.3, SO 9.1–9.3, SD 9.1–9.2)

9.4.1 Challenges

9.4.1.1 Service design

- Dealing with unclear or changing requirements from the business
- Clarifying business requirements and targets for services
- Poor relationships, communications or lack of cooperation between the IT service provider and the business
- Lack of information, monitoring and measurements
- Unreasonable targets and timescales previously agreed in SLAs and OLAs
- Poor supplier management and/or poor supplier performance
- Cost and budgetary constraints
- Determining ROI and the realization of business benefit.

9.4.1.2 Service transition

- Managing contacts, interfaces and relationships across a large customer and stakeholder group
- Lack of harmonization and integration of the supporting processes and disciplines, e.g. finance, engineering, human resources
- Developing standard performance measures and measurement methods across projects and suppliers
- Ensuring that the quality of delivery and support matches the business use of new technology
- Creating an environment that fosters standardization, simplification and knowledge sharing
- Being able to assess, understand the balance and manage risk to IT and risk to the business.

9.4.1.3 Service operation

- Lack of engagement with development and project staff
- Justifying funding on what is often seen as 'infrastructure costs'
- Ensuring the potential impact across all operational services is taken into account in each individual service design and transition
- Ensuring a realistic assessment of true ongoing running costs, after transition, is taken into account in service design
- Ensuring service transition is effective in managing the transition from design to operation
- Understanding what and how to measure to demonstrate good performance
- Being increasingly involved in virtual or matrix teams can lead to confusion over accountability to ensure specific activities are carried out.

9.4.2 Critical success factors

9.4.2.1 Service design

- Understanding business requirements and priorities and that they are taken into account when designing processes and services
- Ensuring good, ongoing communications with the affected individuals
- Involving as many people as possible in the design
- Gaining commitment from senior management as well as from all levels of staff.

9.4.2.2 Service transition

- Understanding the different stakeholder perspectives that underpin effective risk management and maintaining commitment
- Maintaining contact and managing all relationships
- Integrating with other lifecycle stages, processes and disciplines that impact service transition
- Maintaining new and updated knowledge in a form that can be found and used
- Building a thorough understanding of risks that have impacted or may impact successful service transition of services in the service portfolio.

9.4.2.3 Service operation

- Ensuring senior management support is critical for maintaining required funding and resources, as well as visible support when new initiatives are launched
- Ensuring business units understand the role they play in adhering to policies, processes and procedures – such as using the service desk to log all requests
- Training service management staff to an appropriate level of understanding of the business, processes and tools

- Ensuring the suitability and ongoing funding for tools
- Clearly defining how things will be measured and reported – to provide staff with targets to aim for and to allow IT and business managers to review progress and identify opportunities for improvement.

9.4.3   Risks

Many risks are simply the opposite of critical success factors, but the ultimate risk to the business is the loss of critical IT services, with its subsequent adverse impact on employees, customers and finances.

9.4.3.1   Service design

- If any of the prerequisites for success (PFS) are not met then service design will not be successful
- If maturity levels for one process are low, it will be impossible to reach full maturity in other related processes
- Business requirements are not clear to IT staff
- An incorrect balance is struck between innovation, risk and cost while seeking a competitive edge, where desired by the business
- Business timescales do not allow sufficient time for proper service design
- The fit between infrastructure, customers and partners is not sufficient to meet overall business requirements
- A coordinated interface is not available between IT planners and business planners
- Policies and strategies are not available or clearly understood
- There are insufficient resources and budget available for service design activities.

9.4.3.2 Service transition

- Change in accountabilities, responsibilities and practices of existing projects that demotivate the workforce
- Alienation of some key support and operations staff
- Additional, unplanned costs to services in transition
- Resistance to change and circumvention of the processes due to perceived bureaucracy
- Poor integration between processes causing process isolation and a 'silo' approach to delivering ITSM
- Loss of productive hours, higher costs, loss of revenue or perhaps even business failure as a result of poor service transition processes.

9.4.3.3 Service operation

- Ultimate risk to the business is the loss of critical IT services, with a subsequent adverse impact on employees, customers and finances
- If the initial design is faulty, a successful implementation will never give the required results – and redesign will ultimately be necessary
- Inadequate funding and resources available to maintain the infrastructure in a condition to guarantee ongoing service delivery
- Loss of momentum in the implementation of service management due to day-to-day operational tasks taking priority
- Resistance to change due to a reluctance to take new things on board
- Service management being viewed with suspicion by either IT or business
- Differing customer expectations.

9.5 PLANNING AND IMPLEMENTING SERVICE MANAGEMENT TECHNOLOGIES (SO 8.5)

There are a number of factors to consider when deploying and implementing ITSM support tools:

- **Licences** The cost of service management tools is usually determined by the type and number of user licences needed. Most tools are modular, so the specific selection of modules also affects the price. Planning licences is important to avoid unexpected costs. There are a number of different licence types:
  - **Dedicated licences** For staff who need frequent and prolonged use of the module (for example, service desk staff)
  - **Shared licences** For staff who regularly use the module, with significant times when it is not needed. Ratio of licences to users should be calculated to give sufficient use at acceptable cost
  - **Web licences** For staff who need occasional access, or remote access, or only need limited functionality
  - **Service on demand** Charge is based on number of hours the service is used. Suitable for smaller organizations or very specialized tools that are not used often. Can also include tools licensed as part of a consulting exercise (for example, for carrying out capacity modelling)

- **Deployment** Many tools, especially discovery and event monitoring tools, require deployment of clients or agents. This requires careful scheduling, planning and execution and should be subject to formal release and deployment management. Devices may need to be rebooted and this should be planned. Change management should be used and the CMS should be updated. Particular care should be given to planning deployment to laptops and other portable equipment which may not be connected all the time

- **Capacity checks** It may be necessary to check for sufficient system resources (disk space, CPU, memory etc.) when planning a deployment. Allow sufficient lead time for upgrading or replacing equipment. Also check network capacity

- **Timing of technology deployment** If tools are deployed too early then they can be seen as 'the solution' and essential process improvements may not be carried out. If tools are deployed too late then it can be hard to deploy the new process. People need to be trained in the use of the tool, as well as the new or updated process, and timing for this must be planned, possibly with additional training after the tools have gone live

- **Type of introduction** Often the new tool is a replacement for an existing tool, and careful planning is needed for the transition. A phased approach is often more appropriate than a 'big bang' approach, but this depends on the exact circumstances. The key factor is planning what data needs to be migrated, and how. If data is being migrated then a data quality audit should be performed. An alternative approach is parallel running, in which case the old tool should run in a 'read only' mode to prevent mistakes.

10 Qualifications

10.1 OVERVIEW

The ITIL V3 Qualification Scheme has four levels:

- Foundation level
- Intermediate level (Lifecycle and Capability streams)
- ITIL Expert
- ITIL Master.

Candidates gain credits for each examination taken, leading to an ITIL Expert certificate (22 credits). The ITIL Master certificate is in development.

Figure 10.1 The ITIL V3 Qualification Scheme

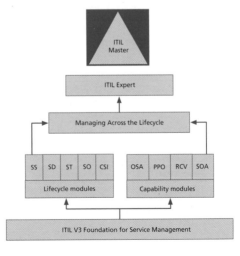

10.2 FOUNDATION

The foundation level ensures candidates gain knowledge of the ITIL terminology, structure and basic concepts, and comprehend the core principles of ITIL practices for service management. Foundation represents two credits towards the ITIL Expert.

10.3 INTERMEDIATE LEVEL

There are two streams in the intermediate level, assessing an individual's ability to analyse and apply concepts of ITIL:

- **Lifecycle stream** Built around the five core publications, for candidates wanting to gain knowledge within the service lifecycle context. Each module achieves three credits
- **Capability stream** Built around the four practitioner-based clusters, for candidates wanting to gain knowledge of specific processes and roles. Each module achieves four credits:
  - **Operational support and analysis** Including event, incident, problem and access management, and request fulfilment processes; service desk, technical, IT operations and application management functions
  - **Planning, protection and optimization** Including capacity, availability, service continuity, information security and demand management processes
  - **Release, control and validation** Including change, release and deployment, service asset and configuration, and knowledge management, request fulfilment, service validation and testing, and evaluation processes
  - **Service offerings and agreement** Including service portfolio, service level, service catalogue, demand, supplier and financial management.

Candidates may take units from either of the streams to accumulate credits.

To complete the intermediate level, the Managing Across the Lifecycle course (five credits) is required to bring together the full essence of a lifecycle approach to service management, consolidating knowledge gained across the qualification scheme.

10.4 ITIL EXPERT

Candidates automatically qualify for an ITIL Expert certificate once they have achieved the pre-requisite 22 credits from foundation (mandatory initial unit) and intermediate units (including Managing Across the Lifecycle, mandatory final unit). No further examinations or courses are required.

10.5 ITIL MASTER

The highest qualification available within the V3 Qualification Scheme, the ITIL Master is reserved for those individuals who can demonstrate and provide evidence of their ability to implement defined ITIL disciplines and ITSM best practices within the real-world working environment.

The ITIL Master qualification is aimed at people who are experienced in the industry – typically, but not exclusively, senior practitioners, senior consultants, senior managers or executives, with five or more years' relevant experience. All candidates must hold the ITIL Expert qualification.

Candidates for the ITIL Master qualification must select one or more real-world situations and explain how they were able to apply their knowledge of ITIL to implement real solutions. Testing is performed by assessing a written submission describing real-world assignments, augmented by oral examination.

10.6 EXISTING ITIL V1 AND V2 QUALIFICATIONS

The ITIL V3 Qualification Scheme has bridging courses for those candidates with existing ITIL (V1 and V2) qualifications. An existing ITIL V1 or V2 Foundation qualification equates to 1.5 credits, and successfully passing a V3 Foundation Bridge course provides the further 0.5 credits required to progress to the intermediate level.

Figure 10.2 The ITIL V3 Bridging Qualification Scheme

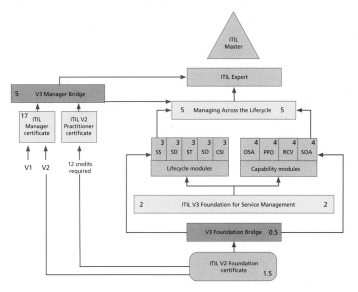

A V1 or V2 Manager qualification equates to 17 credits, and successfully passing a V3 Manager Bridge course provides the further five credits required to achieve the ITIL Expert certificate.

There are also credits for the V2 practitioners, either 2 credits for single processes or 3.5 for clustered processes. A candidate with more than 12 credits from foundation and V2 practitioner courses may take the V3 Manager Bridge and the Managing Across the Lifecycle exams to qualify as an ITIL Expert. Candidates with fewer practitioner credits may combine these with ITIL V3 Lifecycle and Capability exams, and Managing Across the Lifecycle, to achieve ITIL Expert.

There are also complementary qualifications that are awarded credits under this scheme. The number of credits for each qualification can be found in the credit profiler at:

www.itil-officialsite.com/itilservices/V1/map.asp

Note that ITIL V2 is being withdrawn. Removal of V2 will complete on 30 June 2011. Specific product withdrawal dates are:

- V2 Foundation ceased on 30 June 2010
- V2 Manager ceased on 31 August 2010
- V2 Practitioner to cease on 31 December 2010
- Foundation Bridge to cease on 31 December 2010
  (All of the above will be available for resits until
  30 June 2011.)
- Manager Bridge to cease on 30 June 2011.

Once the bridging qualifications are unavailable, candidates will need to attain required service credits and prerequisites via the ITIL V3 Qualification Scheme.

Further information

RELATED STANDARDS AND OTHER SOURCES

ITIL provides advice and guidance on best practice relating to the provision of IT services. The following public frameworks and standards are relevant:

- ISO/IEC 20000: IT Service Management
- ISO/IEC 27001: Information Security Management (ISO/IEC 17799 is the corresponding code of practice)
- ISO/IEC 14001: Environmental Management
- ISO/IEC 15504: Software Process Improvement and Capability Determination (SPICE)
- ISO/IEC 19770 (software asset management)
- ISO/IEC 38500 (governance)
- Capability Maturity Model Integration (CMMI®)
- Control Objectives for Information and related Technology (COBIT®)
- Projects in Controlled Environments (PRINCE2™)
- Project Management Body of Knowledge (PMBOK®)
- Management of Risk (M_o_R®)
- eSourcing Capability Model for Service Providers (eSCM-SP™)
- Telecom Operations Map (eTOM®)
- Six Sigma™.

Organizations need to integrate guidance from multiple frameworks and standards.

The primary standard for IT service management is ISO/IEC 20000. The standard and ITIL are aligned and continue to be aligned, although the standard is being extended and currently includes the following parts:

- ISO/IEC 20000-1:2005 Part 1: Specification (defines the requirements for service management)
- ISO/IEC 20000-2:2005 Part 2: Code of Practice (provides guidance and recommendations on how to meet the requirements in part 1)
- ISO/IEC 20000 TR 2000-3:2009 Part 3: Scoping and Applicability (provides guidance on scope definition and applicability of ISO/IEC 20000-1)
- ISO/IEC 20000-4 Part 4: Service Management Process Reference Model (not available yet)
- ISO/IEC TR 20000-5: 2010 Part 5: An Exemplar Implementation Plan (provides guidance to service providers on how to implement a service management system to fulfil the requirements of ISO/IEC 20000 Part 1)
- BIP 0005: A Manager's Guide to Service Management
- BIP 0015: IT Service Management: Self-assessment Workbook (currently assesses against ITIL V2, to be revised via ITIL V3 complementary publications).

These documents provide a standard against which organizations can be assessed and certified with regard to the quality of their IT service management processes.

An ISO/IEC 20000 certification scheme was designed by itSMF UK and introduced in December 2005. A number of auditing organizations are accredited within the scheme to assess and certify organizations as compliant to the ISO/IEC 20000 standard and its content.

FURTHER GUIDANCE AND CONTACT POINTS

TSO

PO Box 29
Norwich NR3 1GN
United Kingdom
Tel: +44(0) 870 600 5522
Fax: +44(0) 870 600 5533
Email: customer.services@tso.co.uk
www.tso.co.uk

OGC

Rosebery Court
St Andrews Business Park
Norwich NR7 0HS
United Kingdom
Tel: +44(0) 845 000 4999
Email: ServiceDesk@ogc.gsi.gov.uk
www.itil-officialsite.com

itSMF Ltd

150 Wharfedale Road
Winnersh Triangle
Wokingham
Berkshire RG41 5RB
United Kingdom
Tel: +44(0) 118 918 6500
Fax: +44(0) 118 969 9749
Email: publications@itsmf.co.uk
www.itsmf.co.uk

APM Group Limited

Sword House
Totteridge Road
High Wycombe
Buckinghamshire HP13 6DG
United Kingdom
Tel: +44(0) 1494 452 450
Fax: +44(0) 1494 459 559
Email: servicedesk@apmgroupltd.com
www.apmgroupltd.com

Best practice with ITIL

The ITIL V3 publication portfolio consists of a unique library of titles that offer guidance on quality IT services and best practices. These titles include:

- The ITIL lifecycle suite (core publications) which comprises:
    - *Service Strategy*
    - *Service Design*
    - *Service Transition*
    - *Service Operation*
    - *Continual Service Improvement*
    - *Introduction to the ITIL Service Lifecycle*
- Key element guides (pocket-sized reference books based on the core publications)
- *Passing your ITIL Foundation Exam*
- *Passing your ITIL Intermediate Exams*
- *An Introductory Overview of ITIL V3*
- *ITIL V3 Foundation Handbook*
- *Operational Support and Analysis ITIL V3 Intermediate Capability Handbook*
- *Planning, Protection and Optimization ITIL V3 Intermediate Capability Handbook*

- *Release, Control and Validation ITIL V3 Intermediate Capability Handbook*
- *Service Offerings and Agreements ITIL V3 Intermediate Capability Handbook*

About itSMF

The itSMF is the only truly independent and internationally recognized forum for IT service management professionals worldwide. This not-for-profit organization is a prominent player in the ongoing development and promotion of IT service management best practice, standards and qualifications, and has been since 1991.

Globally, the itSMF now boasts more than 6,000 member companies, blue-chip and public-sector alike, covering in excess of 70,000 individuals spread over 40+ international chapters.

Each chapter is a separate legal entity and is largely autonomous. itSMF International provides an overall steering and support function to existing and emerging chapters. It has its own website at www.itsmfi.org.

The UK chapter has in excess of 16,000 members: it offers a flourishing annual conference, online bookstore, regular regional meetings, special-interest groups and numerous other benefits for members. Its website is at www.itsmf.co.uk.

About the Best Management Practice Partnership

UK government and best practice

The Office of Government Commerce (OGC), as an office of HM Treasury, plays a vital role in developing methodologies, processes and frameworks and establishing these as best practice.

The huge growth in the market for OGC's best-practice guidance is evidence of how highly it is valued – proving that it offers not just theory but workable business solutions. ITIL is now the most widely accepted approach to service management in the world, while PRINCE2 has established itself as a global leader in project management.

OGC, on behalf of the UK government, remains committed to maintaining and developing the guidance. Through an innovative and successful partnering arrangement, OGC is able to ensure that users are supported by high-quality publications, training, qualification schemes and consultancy services.

OGC and its official partners

In 2006, OGC completed an open competitive procurement and appointed The Stationery Office (TSO) as official publisher and the APM Group Ltd (APMG) as official accreditor. Together they have created Best Management Practice as the official home of OGC's best-practice guidance. The partners are committed to delivering, supporting and endorsing the very best products and services in the marketplace.

The Stationery Office (TSO)

TSO draws upon more than 200 years of print and publishing services experience, and is the only official publisher for OGC's best-practice guidance.

TSO also manages the various refresh projects on OGC's behalf and ensures that the quality of the guidance is maintained at the highest possible level. A dedicated team serves the Best Management Practice community, providing newsletters, updates and latest information on the products and current projects.

APM Group (APMG)

APMG is a global business providing accreditation and certification services. It is one of the first medium-sized companies to establish an independent Ethics and Standards Board to monitor its business practice and to help ensure it supports the industries it serves in a transparent and responsible way.

APMG has been instrumental in helping to establish PRINCE2 as an international standard and now provides global accreditation schemes in ITIL, PRINCE2, MSP™ (Managing Successful Programmes) and M_o_R (Management of Risk).

Keep up to date with Best Management Practice

The Best Management Practice Knowledge Centre brings together the official partners and recognized user groups to create a comprehensive source of information. Here you can find articles, White Papers, book reviews and events, as well as links to the individual product sites.

Visit www.best-management-practice.com

Glossary

A candidate is expected to understand the following terms after completing an SOA course.

These terms are as defined in the standard ITIL glossary. Those terms with an asterisk (*) are not defined in the current version of the glossary, but a summary definition for the term has been provided for revision purposes.

The core publication titles (*Service Strategy, Service Design, Service Operation, Service Transition, Continual Service Improvement*) included in parentheses at the beginning of the definition indicate where a reader can find more information.

acceptance
Formal agreement that an IT service, process, plan or other deliverable is complete, accurate, reliable and meets its specified requirements. Acceptance is usually preceded by evaluation or testing and is often required before proceeding to the next stage of a project or process.

agreed service time
(*Service Design*) A synonym for service hours, commonly used in formal calculations of availability. *See also* downtime.

agreement
A document that describes a formal understanding between two or more parties. An agreement is not legally binding, unless it forms part of a contract. *See also* operational level agreement; service level agreement.

availability
(Service Design) Ability of an IT service or other configuration item to perform its agreed function when required. Availability is determined by reliability, maintainability, serviceability, performance and security. Availability is usually calculated as a percentage. This calculation is often based on agreed service time and downtime. It is best practice to calculate availability of an IT service using measurements of the business output.

availability plan
(Service Design) A plan to ensure that existing and future availability requirements for IT services can be provided cost-effectively.

balanced scorecard
(Continual Service Improvement) A management tool developed by Drs Robert Kaplan (Harvard Business School) and David Norton. A balanced scorecard enables a strategy to be broken down into key performance indicators. Performance against the KPIs is used to demonstrate how well the strategy is being achieved. A balanced scorecard has four major areas, each of which has a small number of KPIs. The same four areas are considered at different levels of detail throughout the organization.

business capacity management
(Service Design) In the context of ITSM, business capacity management is the activity responsible for understanding future business requirements for use in the capacity plan. *See also* service capacity management.

business case
(Service Strategy) Justification for a significant item of expenditure. The business case includes information about costs, benefits, options, issues, risks and possible problems.

business impact analysis

(Service Strategy) Business impact analysis is the activity in business continuity management that identifies vital business functions and their dependencies. These dependencies may include suppliers, people, other business processes, IT services etc. Business impact analysis defines the recovery requirements for IT services. These requirements include recovery time objectives, recovery point objectives and minimum service level targets for each IT service.

business relationship management

The process or function responsible for maintaining a relationship with the business. Business relationship management usually includes:

- Managing personal relationships with business managers
- Carrying out demand management activities
- Providing input to product managers for use in service portfolio management
- Ensuring that the IT service provider is satisfying the business needs of the customers

This process has strong links with service level management.

business relationship manager

(Service Strategy) A role responsible for maintaining the relationship with one or more customers. This role is often combined with the service level manager role.

business service catalogue*

(Service Design) A customer-facing view of the service catalogue. Information about all live customer-facing IT services, including those available for deployment, will be visible through the business service catalogue. This view is the only part of the service portfolio available to customers, and is used to support the sale and delivery of IT services. The business service

catalogue includes information about deliverables, prices, contact points, ordering and request processes. *See also* technical service catalogue.

business unit
(Service Strategy) A segment of the business that has its own plans, metrics, income and costs. Each business unit owns assets and uses these to create value for customers in the form of goods and services.

capacity
(Service Design) The maximum throughput that a configuration item or IT service can deliver whilst meeting agreed service level targets. For some types of CI, capacity may be the size or volume, for example a disk drive.

capacity management
(Service Design) The process responsible for ensuring that the capacity of IT services and the IT infrastructure is able to deliver agreed service level targets in a cost-effective and timely manner. Capacity management considers all resources required to deliver the IT service, and plans for short-, medium- and long-term business requirements.

capacity management information system
(Service Design) A virtual repository of all capacity management data, usually stored in multiple physical locations. *See also* service knowledge management system.

capacity plan
(Service Design) A capacity plan is used to manage the resources required to deliver IT services. The plan contains scenarios for different predictions of business demand, and costed options to deliver the agreed service level targets.

capital item
(Service Strategy) An asset that is of interest to financial management because it is above an agreed financial value.

capitalization
(Service Strategy) Identifying major cost as capital, even though no asset is purchased. This is done to spread the impact of the cost over multiple accounting periods. The most common example of this is software development, or purchase of a software licence.

charging
(Service Strategy) Requiring payment for IT services. Charging for IT services is optional, and many organizations choose to treat their IT service provider as a cost centre.

chargeback*
(Service Strategy) An approach to charging for IT services. Different chargeback models can be used that either require payment for the services provided (charging), or inform customers of the costs that have been incurred, but no money is actually transferred (notional charging).

component capacity management
(Continual Service Improvement) (Service Design) The process responsible for understanding the capacity, utilization and performance of configuration items. Data is collected, recorded and analysed for use in the capacity plan. *See also* service capacity management.

configuration item
(Service Transition) Any component that needs to be managed in order to deliver an IT service. Information about each configuration item is recorded in a configuration record within the configuration management system and is maintained

throughout its lifecycle by configuration management. Configuration items are under the control of change management. They typically include IT services, hardware, software, buildings, people and formal documentation such as process documentation and service level agreements.

configuration management system
(Service Transition) A set of tools and databases that are used to manage an IT service provider's configuration data. The configuration management system also includes information about incidents, problems, known errors, changes and releases, and may contain data about employees, suppliers, locations, business units, customers and users. The configuration management system includes tools for collecting, storing, managing, updating and presenting data about all configuration items and their relationships. The configuration management system is maintained by configuration management and is used by all IT service management processes. *See also* service knowledge management system.

contract
A legally binding agreement between two or more parties.

contract portfolio
(Service Strategy) A database or structured document used to manage service contracts or agreements between an IT service provider and its customers. Each IT service delivered to a customer should have a contract or other agreement that is listed in the contract portfolio. *See also* service catalogue; service portfolio.

cost centre
(Service Strategy) A business unit or project to which costs are assigned. A cost centre does not charge for services provided. An IT service provider can be run as a cost centre or a profit centre.

cost element

(Service Strategy) The middle level of category to which costs are assigned in budgeting and accounting. The highest-level category is cost type. For example, a cost type of 'people' could have cost elements of payroll, staff benefits, expenses, training, overtime etc. Cost elements can be further broken down to give cost units. For example, the cost element 'expenses' could include cost units of hotels, transport, meals etc.

cost management

(Service Strategy) A general term that is used to refer to budgeting and accounting, and is sometimes used as a synonym for financial management.

cost type

(Service Strategy) The highest level of category to which costs are assigned in budgeting and accounting – for example, hardware, software, people, accommodation, external and transfer. *See also* cost element; cost unit.

cost unit

(Service Strategy) The lowest level of category to which costs are assigned, cost units are usually things that can be easily counted (e.g. staff numbers, software licences) or things easily measured (e.g. CPU usage, electricity consumed). Cost units are included within cost elements. For example, a cost element of 'expenses' could include cost units of hotels, transport, meals etc. *See also* cost type.

depreciation

(Service Strategy) A measure of the reduction in value of an asset over its life. This is based on wearing out, consumption or other reduction in the useful economic value.

direct cost
(Service Strategy) The cost of providing an IT service which can be allocated in full to a specific customer, cost centre, project etc. For example, the cost of providing non-shared servers or software licences. *See also* indirect cost.

downtime
(Service Design) (Service Operation) The time when an IT service or other configuration item is not available during its agreed service time. The availability of an IT service is often calculated from agreed service time and downtime.

event
(Service Operation) A change of state that has significance for the management of an IT service or other configuration item. The term is also used to mean an alert or notification created by any IT service, configuration item or monitoring tool. Events typically require IT operations personnel to take actions, and often lead to incidents being logged.

external service provider
(Service Strategy) An IT service provider that is part of a different organization from its customer. An IT service provider may have both internal and external customers.

incident
(Service Operation) An unplanned interruption to an IT service or reduction in the quality of an IT service. Failure of a configuration item that has not yet affected service is also an incident – for example, failure of one disk from a mirror set.

indirect cost
(Service Strategy) The cost of providing an IT service which cannot be allocated in full to a specific customer – for example, the cost of providing shared servers or software licences. Also known as overhead. *See also* direct cost.

internal customer
A customer who works for the same business as the IT service provider. *See also* internal service provider.

internal service provider
(Service Strategy) An IT service provider that is part of the same organization as its customer. An IT service provider may have both internal and external customers.

key performance indicator
(Continual Service Improvement) (Service Design) A metric that is used to help manage a process, IT service or activity. Many metrics may be measured, but only the most important of these are defined as key performance indicators and used to actively manage and report on the process, IT service or activity. They should be selected to ensure that efficiency, effectiveness and cost-effectiveness are all managed.

line of service
(Service Strategy) A core service or supporting service that has multiple service level packages. A line of service is managed by a product manager and each service level package is designed to support a particular market segment.

marginal cost
(Service Strategy) The increase or decrease in the cost of producing one more, or one less, unit of output – for example, the cost of supporting an additional user.

mean time between failures
(Service Design) A metric for measuring and reporting reliability. MTBF is the average time that an IT service or other configuration item can perform its agreed function without interruption. This is measured from when the configuration item starts working, until it next fails.

mean time between service incidents
(Service Design) A metric used for measuring and reporting reliability. It is the mean time from when a system or IT service fails, until it next fails. MTBSI is equal to MTBF plus MTRS.

mean time to repair
The average time taken to repair an IT service or other configuration item after a failure. MTTR is measured from when the configuration item fails until it is repaired. MTTR does not include the time required to recover or restore. It is sometimes incorrectly used to mean mean time to restore service.

mean time to restore service
The average time taken to restore an IT service or other configuration item after a failure. MTRS is measured from when the configuration item fails until it is fully restored and delivering its normal functionality. *See also* mean time to repair.

measurement*
The result of measuring.

metric
(Continual Service Improvement) Something that is measured and reported to help manage a process, IT service or activity. *See also* key performance indicator.

monitoring
(Service Operation) Repeated observation of a configuration item, IT service or process to detect events and to ensure that the current status is known.

net present value
(Service Strategy) A technique used to help make decisions about capital expenditure. It compares cash inflows with cash outflows. Positive net present value indicates that an investment is worthwhile. *See also* return on investment.

notional charging

(Service Strategy) An approach to charging for IT services. Charges to customers are calculated and customers are informed of the charge, but no money is actually transferred. Notional charging is sometimes introduced to ensure that customers are aware of the costs they incur, or as a stage during the introduction of real charging.

operational level agreement

(Continual Service Improvement) (Service Design) An agreement between an IT service provider and another part of the same organization. It supports the IT service provider's delivery of IT services to customers and defines the goods or services to be provided and the responsibilities of both parties. For example, there could be an operational level agreement:

- Between the IT service provider and a procurement department to obtain hardware in agreed times
- Between the service desk and a support group to provide incident resolution in agreed times.

See also service level agreement.

opportunity cost

(Service Strategy) A cost that is used in deciding between investment choices. Opportunity cost represents the revenue that would have been generated by using the resources in a different way. For example, the opportunity cost of purchasing a new server may include not carrying out a service improvement activity that the money could have been spent on. Opportunity cost analysis is used as part of a decision-making process, but is not treated as an actual cost in any financial statement.

pattern of business activity
(Service Strategy) A workload profile of one or more business activities. Patterns of business activity are used to help the IT service provider understand and plan for different levels of business activity.

percentage utilization
(Service Design) The amount of time that a component is busy over a given period of time. For example, if a central processing unit is busy for 1,800 seconds in a one-hour period, its utilization is 50%.

planned downtime
(Service Design) Agreed time when an IT service will not be available. Planned downtime is often used for maintenance, upgrades and testing. *See also* downtime.

recovery
(Service Design) (Service Operation) Returning a configuration item or an IT service to a working state. Recovery of an IT service often includes recovering data to a known consistent state. After recovery, further steps may be needed before the IT service can be made available to the users (restoration).

recovery option
(Service Design) A strategy for responding to an interruption to service. Commonly used strategies are: do nothing, manual workaround, reciprocal arrangement, gradual recovery, intermediate recovery, fast recovery, immediate recovery. Recovery options may make use of dedicated facilities or third-party facilities shared by multiple businesses.

redundancy

Use of one or more additional configuration items to provide fault tolerance. The term also has a generic meaning of obsolescence, or no longer needed.

reliability

(Continual Service Improvement) (Service Design) A measure of how long an IT service or other configuration item can perform its agreed function without interruption. Usually measured as MTBF or MTBSI. The term can also be used to state how likely it is that a process, function etc. will deliver its required outputs. *See also* availability.

resilience

(Service Design) The ability of an IT service or other configuration item to resist failure or to recover in a timely manner following a failure. For example, an armoured cable will resist failure when put under stress.

return on investment

(Continual Service Improvement) (Service Strategy) A measurement of the expected benefit of an investment. In the simplest sense, it is the net profit of an investment divided by the net worth of the assets invested. *See also* net present value.

risk

A possible event that could cause harm or loss, or affect the ability to achieve objectives. A risk is measured by the probability of a threat, the vulnerability of the asset to that threat, and the impact it would have if it occurred.

service capacity management

(Continual Service Improvement) (Service Design) The activity responsible for understanding the performance and capacity of IT services. The resources used by each IT service and the pattern

of usage over time are collected, recorded and analysed for use in the capacity plan. *See also* business capacity management; component capacity management.

service catalogue
(Service Design) A database or structured document with information about all live IT services, including those available for deployment. The service catalogue is the only part of the service portfolio published to customers, and is used to support the sale and delivery of IT services. The service catalogue includes information about deliverables, prices, contact points, ordering and request processes. *See also* contract portfolio.

service design
(Service Design) A stage in the lifecycle of an IT service. Service design includes a number of processes and functions and is the title of one of the core ITIL publications.

service design package
(Service Design) Document(s) defining all aspects of an IT service and its requirements through each stage of its lifecycle. A service design package is produced for each new IT service, major change or IT service retirement.

service hours
(Continual Service Improvement) (Service Design) An agreed time period when a particular IT service should be available. For example, 'Monday–Friday 08:00 to 17:00 except public holidays'. Service hours should be defined in a service level agreement.

service investment analysis*
(Service Strategy) An activity that analyses the expected value or return on investment that will be derived from an IT service over its lifecycle. Service investment analysis is an activity within financial management.

service knowledge management system

(Service Transition) A set of tools and databases that are used to manage knowledge and information. The service knowledge management system includes the configuration management system, as well as other tools and databases. It stores, manages, updates and presents all information that an IT service provider needs to manage the full lifecycle of IT services.

service level agreement

(Continual Service Improvement) (Service Design) An agreement between an IT service provider and a customer. A service level agreement describes the IT service, documents service level targets, and specifies the responsibilities of the IT service provider and the customer. A single agreement may cover multiple IT services or multiple customers. *See also* operational level agreement.

service level package

(Service Strategy) A defined level of utility and warranty for a particular service package. Each service level package is designed to meet the needs of a particular pattern of business activity. *See also* line of service.

service level requirement

(Continual Service Improvement) (Service Design) A customer requirement for an aspect of an IT service. Service level requirements are based on business objectives and used to negotiate agreed service level targets.

service level target

(Continual Service Improvement) (Service Design) A commitment that is documented in a service level agreement. Service level targets are based on service level requirements, and are needed to ensure that the IT service design is fit for purpose. They should be SMART, and are usually based on key performance indicators.

service manager

A manager who is responsible for managing the end-to-end lifecycle of one or more IT services. The term is also used to mean any manager within the IT service provider. Most commonly used to refer to a business relationship manager, a process manager, an account manager or a senior manager with responsibility for IT services overall.

service measurement*

(Continual Service Improvement) Measuring the performance of services, including availability, reliability and performance. These measures are combined to form an overall view of the customer experience. *See also* measurement.

service measurement framework*

(Continual Service Improvement) A framework of measurements that allows an organization to effectively manage and report on the services that they provide and on the technology and processes that support them. The framework should include several perspectives such as components, services, activities, processes and outputs.

service measurement model*

(Continual Service Improvement) A representation of the multiple levels of measurement within the service measurement framework.

service metrics*

(Continual Service Improvement) The results of the end-to-end service. Component/technology metrics are used to compute the service metrics. *See also* metric.

service package

(Service Strategy) A detailed description of an IT service that is available to be delivered to customers. A service package includes a service level package and one or more core services and supporting services.

service pipeline

(Service Strategy) A database or structured document listing all IT services that are under consideration or development, but are not yet available to customers. The service pipeline provides a business view of possible future IT services and is part of the service portfolio that is not normally published to customers.

service portfolio

(Service Strategy) The complete set of services that are managed by a service provider. The service portfolio is used to manage the entire lifecycle of all services, and includes three categories: service pipeline (proposed or in development), service catalogue (live or available for deployment) and retired services. *See also* contract portfolio.

service provider

(Service Strategy) An organization supplying services to one or more internal customers or external customers. Service provider is often used as an abbreviation for IT service provider.

service reporting

(Continual Service Improvement) The process responsible for producing and delivering reports of achievement and trends against service levels. Service reporting should agree the format, content and frequency of reports with customers.

service request

(Service Operation) A request from a user for information or advice, for a standard change or for access to an IT service – for example, to reset a password or to provide standard IT services for a new user. Service requests are usually handled by a service desk and do not require a request for change to be submitted.

service scorecard*

(Continual Service Improvement) A management tool that provides a snapshot of the performance of a specific service. Service scorecards are maintained as part of service measurement and contribute towards an overall balanced scorecard.

service valuation

(Service Strategy) A measurement of the total cost of delivering an IT service, and the total value to the business of that IT service. Service valuation is used to help the business and the IT service provider agree on the value of the IT service.

stakeholder

All people who have an interest in an organization, project, IT service etc. Stakeholders may be interested in the activities, targets, resources or deliverables. Stakeholders may include customers, partners, employees, shareholders, owners etc.

statement of requirements

(Service Design) A document containing all requirements for a product purchase, or a new or changed IT service. *See also* terms of reference.

supplier

(Service Design) (Service Strategy) A third party responsible for supplying goods or services that are required to deliver IT services. Examples of suppliers include commodity hardware and software vendors, network and telecom providers, and outsourcing organizations. *See also* underpinning contract.

supplier and contract database

(Service Design) A database or structured document used to manage supplier contracts throughout their lifecycle. The supplier and contract database contains key attributes of all contracts with suppliers, and should be part of the service knowledge management system.

supplier management

(Service Design) The process responsible for ensuring that all contracts with suppliers support the needs of the business, and that all suppliers meet their contractual commitments.

technical service catalogue*

(Service Design) An internal service provider's view of the service catalogue. Information about all live IT services, including those available for deployment, will be visible through this view, such as details of the relationship between customer-facing IT services and other supporting or infrastructure services. *See also* business service catalogue.

terms of reference

(Service Design) A document specifying the requirements, scope, deliverables, resources and schedule for a project or activity.

throughput

(Service Design) A measure of the number of transactions or other operations performed in a fixed time – for example, 5,000 e-mails sent per hour, or 200 disk I/Os per second.

total cost of ownership
(Service Strategy) A methodology used to help make investment decisions. It assesses the full lifecycle cost of owning a configuration item, not just the initial cost or purchase price. *See also* total cost of utilization.

total cost of utilization
(Service Strategy) A methodology used to help make investment and service sourcing decisions. Total cost of utilization assesses the full lifecycle cost to the customer of using an IT service. *See also* total cost of ownership.

underpinning contract
(Service Design) A contract between an IT service provider and a third party. The third party provides goods or services that support delivery of an IT service to a customer. The underpinning contract defines targets and responsibilities that are required to meet agreed service level targets in a service level agreement.

usability
(Service Design) The ease with which an application, product or IT service can be used. Usability requirements are often included in a statement of requirements.

utility
(Service Strategy) Functionality offered by a product or service to meet a particular need. Utility is often summarized as 'what it does', and may be used as a synonym for service utility.

variable cost dynamics
(Service Strategy) A technique used to understand how overall costs are affected by the many complex variable elements that contribute to the provision of IT services.

warranty
(Service Strategy) A promise or guarantee that a product or service will meet its agreed requirements. Warranty is often used as a synonym for service warranty.